Edinburgh Curiosities 2

JAMES U THOMSON

JOHN DONALD PUBLISHERS LTD
EDINBURGH

© James U. Thomson 1997

All rights reserved.

No part of this publication may be reproduced
in any form or by any means without
the prior permission of the publishers
John Donald Publishers Limited,
138 St Stephen Street, Edinburgh, EH3 5AA.

ISBN 0 85976 479 6

British Library Cataloguing in Publication Data.

A catalogue record for this book is available
from the British Library.

Except where otherwise stated,
photographs are by the author.

Typesetting & prepress origination by Brinnoven, Livingston.
Printed & bound in Great Britain by Bell & Bain Ltd, Glasgow.

CONTENTS

ACKNOWLEDGEMENTS

In compiling this second volume of Edinburgh Curiosities I have received a great deal of assistance from a number of individuals and establishments, and to all I offer my sincere thanks and gratitude.

George Watson's College, and the college librarian, Fiona Hooper, were most helpful in allowing me to photograph the 'zeppelin' plaque erected as a reminder of the 1916 air raid, and for the use of the two photographs showing the war damage to the former college building in Archibald Place.

Nina Sobecka, of the National Trust for Scotland, willingly provided the material relating to the Trust's interest in Charlotte Square.

With regard to the Catherine Sinclair drinking fountain, my trail dried up in the 1960s when I last saw it dismantled and stacked in a corner of the former Edinburgh Corporation's yard in Russell Road. But thanks to the efforts of Ian Temple, City of Edinburgh Council, it was possible to track its movements to the now permanent location adjacent to the Water of Leith Walkway.

In a casual conversation with Brian Sibbald, archivist at St Mary's RC Cathedral, I discovered that the Cathedral records included pictures which illustrate, very clearly, how dangerously close the Cathedral was to the Theatre Royal building. This resulted in considerable damage to the Cathedral structure caused by a series of fires which broke out in the theatre over a number of years when, perhaps, safety standards did not meet the high level demanded today. For the use of the Cathedral/Theatre Royal pictures of yesteryears I am grateful to the Revd Father Gemmell (the Cathedral Administer), and Brian Sibbald the Archivist.

The staff at West Register House were most courteous and helpful in making available the papers relating to the zeppelin raid, and, as ever, the staff at the Edinburgh Room, Central Library, George IV Bridge, assisted in solving several problems.

I was aware of the story concerning the Queen Victoria gravestones at Rosebank, but the big question was — where were they located in what, after all, is a relative large cemetery? They were traced by my daughter Heather, who did a systematic 'trawl' of the graveyard and found the answer. Heather also offered some constructive criticism in addition to assisting with proofreading. Finally, to Brenda my wife, a big thank you for the patient hours she spent in various tasks which resulted in this second volume of Edinburgh Curiosities being completed.

James U. Thomson
Edinburgh
1997

– 1 –
EDINBURGH: AND THE OPINION
OF 18TH-CENTURY VISITORS

The visitor is spoiled for choice when it comes to the holiday-guide. There is a wide and varied selection available from the small, cheap and handy publication which will slip easily into a pocket, to the more expensive volume complete with coloured photographs. But in one respect they are similar, basically following the same formula.

Guidebooks, of course, are not a product of the modern era; they have been around for centuries, and many years ago I had occasion to consult one such publication which had been produced by T. Brown, North Bridge Street, Edinburgh, in 1792. This 118-page book contained a brief history of the town, description of the buildings and general information relating to transport facilities and postal services.

In 1621, the book records, a law was passed whereby houses which previously had been roofed with straw or boards were required to be covered with slates, tiles or lead. Seventy-seven years later a further regulation came into being which restricted the height of buildings to five storeys. Street lighting also received the attention of the magistrates who, in 1684, directed that candles were to be hung from the first floor window of every house. Also, in that year it was agreed that two coaches and eight horses be purchased for the use of the magistrates; and women were forbidden to wear shawls over their heads. The penalty for defying this law was a fine of £5 and forfeiture of the shawl. A third offence could be punished with banishment.

The list of places worthy of a visit is surprisingly familiar and included the castle, St Giles' Cathedral, Parliament House, Register House, Canongate Church, the High School and Holyrood. Also included were Heriot's Hospital, Watson's Hospital, the Merchant Maiden Hospital, Trades Maiden Hospital and the Orphan Hospital (which stood roughly in the vicinity of the GPO building).

Visitors were informed that the infirmary was attended by two physicians chosen by the managers. They visited the hospital

1

daily, but all members of the College of Surgeons attended in rotation. Statistics were obviously not issued too frequently as those quoted related to the year 1782 when 6,370 patients were admitted. Of those who crossed the hospital portals, 4,395 were cured, 358 died, and the others were relieved of their ailments, dismissed as incurable, left of their own accord or remained in the infirmary.

The Assembly Rooms , not long open, were recommended as a meeting place, and here, for a fee of five shillings, visitors could play cards or dance under the direction of a master of ceremonies. It was proudly boasted that the largest room in the suite, which was 100 feet long and 40 feet broad, was the second largest of its kind in Britain.

On the road to Leith stood the Amphitheatre, which had been opened in 1790 for equestrian exhibitions, pantomimes and dancing. The entertainment provided at this establishment was described as being on a par with that seen in London. It also served as a riding school.

The theatre would be found in Shakespeare Square (GPO site) and although described as a plain building on the outside, it was elegantly fitted within. These premises were open on three evenings a week.

In the High Street, visitors could see the Tolbooth, which was erected in 1561 and housed the prison, Parliament offices and the courts. It was delicately pointed out, however, that this building had become unfit for habitation and was to be demolished. The Lord Provost was Captain of the Tolbooth, although administration was conducted by a jailer. The latter had sole responsibility for obtaining all provisions for the prisoners, 'a circumstance', the guide-book pointed out 'which must certainly be considered as a grievous oppression, those who are least able to purchase them being thus obliged to do so at the highest price'.

Forrest Road now passes through what was the Charity Workhouse site. This institution was erected in 1743 and housed 700 residents and 300 out-workers. Each was allowed to retain two pence of every shilling earned. The authorities had one problem; the expenditure for running the establishment had been set at £4,000 per annum, but they found that it required £4:10/- a head to provide the necessities of life!

Edinburgh had a population of 100,000 in 1792, but the Town

Guard only consisted of three officers and 90 other ranks. They were dressed in similar fashion to soldiers and when called to quell a mob they were provided with Lochaber-axes.

The officers received the same pay as an army lieutenant and the rank-and-file were paid in accordance with their army equivalent rank. The upkeep of this organisation was met from a tax levied on the tradesmen. This, however, produced only £1,250 and the balance had to be provided by the magistrates.

Letters to England left the town each day except Thursday at 3.30 p.m. and arrived three days later. The charge was seven pence. Mail to North America and the West Indies was made up on the Saturday preceding the first Wednesday of every month. The cost was one shilling and seven pence and had to be paid in advance if addressed to a North American resident, but letters to the West Indies were accepted COD.

Public transport consisted of a half-hourly horse-drawn vehicle service which operated between the Cross and Leith Shore; the fare was four-and-a-half pence. Four coaches a day, except Sunday, operated between the town and Dalkeith at a cost of one shilling and threepence. Other fares were Musselburgh 1 shilling, Haddington 4 shillings, Peebles 5 shillings, Glasgow between 8 shillings and 12/6, Perth 11/6, Aberdeen £2:2/-, Jedburgh 11/6, Kelso 13/-, Linlithgow 3/6 and Falkirk 5/-.

The Edinburgh-London Royal Mail set out from St Andrew Street each afternoon at 3.30 and was at Newcastle by nine o'clock next morning.

It was due in York at 4 p.m. the same day and was in London by 5 a.m. on the third day after leaving the Scottish capital. The fare was £1:16/-to Newcastle and £6:6/- to London.

Hackney carriages were available in the town at a cost of sixpence for a local journey, but to Leith the charge was two shillings and sixpence. An extra sixpence was asked for a night journey. A weekly 'runabout' hire was 25 shillings.

Porters could be hired very readily, and charged three shillings to transport twelve hundredweights of coal to the fourth floor or above, two shillings and two pence to the third level and two shillings below this point. They would carry articles (except wine and furniture) to any part of the town for one shilling.

And this guide to Edinburgh had one final word of assurance for the visitor, claiming that 'no city in the world can afford greater security to the inhabitants in their person and properties than Edinburgh'.

Through the Eyes of a Glaswegian

The journey between Glasgow and Edinburgh is, today, a not too harrowing experience. There is an adequate train service and, traffic congestion and road works permitting, the trip by road can be completed in a reasonable time — usually. Yes, there are problems, but nothing compared to the nightmare which one Glasgow man was subjected to in 1784: he was thirteen hours on the road!

Our visitor, who was making his first trip to Edinburgh as a guest of a minister friend, had an early start from his home in order to reach the Saracen's Head Inn in the Gallowgate, where the chaise and pair to Edinburgh departed daily at 7 a.m. The journey to join the coach was made on foot, and on the way he passed Gabriel Watson's quarters where a great six-wheeled coach drawn by eight horses was already being unloaded. It was the London to Glasgow stage which had just arrived after an arduous journey.

The two horses were harnessed and with no delay the coach left on time. It was a slow journey, however, and never exceeded six miles an hour, but even this pace dropped on the slightest hill. Cumbernauld was reached in two hours and at this point a stop was made, lasting one-and-a-half hours, to enable the passengers to have breakfast and allow the horses to be rested. The next stop was Linlithgow at 2 p.m. with time for a late lunch and a look around the town before departing at 3.30 p.m.

Although the horses had been replaced, the speed did not increase, and after continuing for two hours, yet another halt was made, this time at a wayside inn where tea was taken and the animals rested. At approximately 8 p.m. the horses pulled to a stop in the Grassmarket — the ordeal was over.

Wherever Edinburgh and Glasgow people meet, sooner or later discussion will turn to the merits of the respective towns. But this is nothing new and the 18th-century Glaswegian made no secret of his opinion of Edinburgh. He deplored the attitude that Edinburgh people considered themselves better bred than their Glasgow cousins and there was no doubt in his mind that Glasgow was the better town.

'Our Trongate', he wrote, 'beat the High Street; our High

Church was grander by thousands than their Holyrood,; our St Andrew's Church was better than their St Giles'…and as for their college, it was a poor shabby affair and our college beat it to atoms.' Even Parliament House did not escape the caustic words of the writer and he described it as little better than Glasgow's Tontine. It was conceded that Glasgow did not have long streets which were as new as Princes Street or George Street.

A castle Glasgow did not have, but not to be outdone, our visitor was firm in his belief that if a large house was constructed in Craig's Park 'it would look as pretty a place as the castle'. The Mound was a 'shapeless mass and scarcely passable for glaur and nastiness' while the Nor' Loch was nothing but a swamp, full of the waste from Castlehill, Lawnmarket, High Street and the Luckenbooths. The dirty meadows was a most atrocious place, smelling from stagnant water and other filth collected from Bristo Street, Potter Row, George Square, Lauriston and Sciennes. Indeed they were quite incomparable with the beautiful Clyde or noble Glasgow Green.

The Cowgate, Potter Row and Candlemaker's Row were acceptable, but certainly no better than Glasgow's Bridgegate, or its wynds and vennels.

The Calton Hill — not a match for Ratten Raw, while a walk along Princes Street, although impressive, was not as grand as the walks along Trongate and Saltmarket. The West Bow and Nether Bow were, he thought, curious but twenty times better was Deanside Brae or Bell o' the Brae in Glasgow. And how troublesome to climb the steep slopes of Arthur's Seat to see the panoramic view of the town which, after all, did not surpass the sight from Cathkin Braes — 'and we make no brag about the matter!'

Was this Glaswegian poking fun or did he honestly believe that his town was superior to the Scottish capital? That we will never know, but perhaps it was a good thing that Edinburgh and Glasgow were a thirteen hours' journey apart!

And as an Englishman Saw the Town

Two hundred years ago the idea of a trip from the south of England was a venture not considered lightly, but some adventurists took the right decision, boarded a stage-coach for Edinburgh and were suitably impressed.

5

Writing of such a visit in 1771, one southerner, seeing the town for the first time, described it as 'a city that possess a boldness and grandeur of situation beyond any that I have ever seen...the view of the houses at a distance strikes the traveller with wonder; their own loftiness, improved by their almost aerial situation, gives them a look of magnificence not to be found in any other part of Great Britain.'

Despite the awe-inspiring height of some of the houses (the back of one tenement built on a slope was twelve or thirteen storeys) the circumstances whereby several families sharing a common stair did not impress our visitor. Nevertheless, he confessed, the cleanliness within these stairways was, generally speaking, fairly high. The streets were cleaned early each morning, but the inhabitants of some closes and alleys had not yet been convinced that it was not in the interest of public health to deposit filth in the streets. With the familiar phrase 'gardez-l'eau' they would show little respect for the unsuspecting passer-by as the rubbish was thrown from the upper windows. It was little comfort for the unfortunate victim that 'the sufferer may call every inhabitant of the house it came from to account and make them prove the delinquent'. The magistrates dealt severely with any culprits.

Edinburgh Castle, St Giles', Parliament House and Holyrood were, as they are today, great attractions for visitors, but there was much to be seen which can no longer be viewed by the present-day tourist. The Luckenbooths, Tolbooth Prison and guard-house in the High Street were popular attractions, although our visitor expressed the opinion that the location of the last two buildings served only to spoil 'as fine a street as most in Europe'. The High Street was finely built, he admitted, and its width (eighty feet in some places) left a lasting impression. And the English traveller was surprised to find on a church visit that there was no music.

The Royal Exchange (now the City Chambers) was the source of great amusement. Built between 1753 and 1761 for the benefit mainly of the city merchants, they clung to their old ways and continued to conduct their business in the open. Even the huge cistern on the Castlehill was considered to be something worth seeing. This container held about 230 tons of water which was conveyed from the Pentland Hills and formed the main water supply for the town. In the Grassmarket, visitors were shown where cattle were sold — and criminals hanged!

The university was a modest building and accommodated 600 students. They were subjected to no regulations yet proved to be most conscientious and few let the college down. Classes were conducted by 22 professors who were most able men, particularly those in the medical field. The infirmary had beds for 200 patients and was equipped with an operating theatre.

In close proximity an area of 27 acres had been earmarked for the building of George Square. It was partly developed, with small commodious houses built in the English style. Such was the spirit of development at this period, that in three years, £80,000 had been spent on house building. On the north side of the city, the New Town was under construction and was a great attraction

The houses in St Andrew Square were selling at a price of between £1,800 and £2,000. Some of the grander accommodation, however, was also available, but these exclusive properties were on the market at between £4,000 and £5,000. This project, the Englishman admitted, 'is planned with great judgement and will prove a great and magnificent addition to Edinburgh'.

In the markets, pigeons were on sale at between eight pence and five shillings a dozen, chickens cost between eight pence and one shilling a pair, a fowl one shilling and two pence, a large turkey was four or five shillings and a pig the princely sum of two shillings. Coal was available at between five and six pence a hundred-weight — delivered.

For short walks within the town, Arthur's Seat and Salisbury Crags were popular. From the top of Calton Hill visitors could gaze into a deep and wide hollow where, in earlier years, witches and sorcerers were burned at the stake.

Excursions within easy reach of the town included Craigmillar Castle, Newbattle, Dalkeith — and Leith. The latter was described as 'dirty, ill-built and chiefly inhabited by sailors'. Our English visitor had at least some respect for the inhabitants of the Port, however, for he noticed that the Leith Races, which were held on the sands near low water mark, were poorly attended — a proof that dissipation has not generally infected the manners of the North Britons'.

Captain Topham: Temporary Resident

It is wrong for anyone to pass judgement on a city on the basis of an excursion visit.

Perhaps one of the best assessments of eighteenth-century Edinburgh can be gleaned from the letters of Captain Topham, which were written between 1774 and 1775. Topham was a seasoned traveller with a wide experience of conditions and facilities in many parts of Europe. Unfortunately, Topham's immediate reaction on his arrival in the Scottish capital was one of shock:

> One can scarcely form in imagination the distress of a miserable stranger on his first entrance into the city as there is no inn that is better than an alehouse, nor any accommodation that is decent, clean or fit to receive a gentleman.

Topham, an Englishman, had arrived in the Pleasance accompanied by a travelling companion. They were received by a poorly-clad girl without shoes or stockings, and taken to a room where about twenty drovers were devouring a meal of whisky and potatoes. No beds were available, but the visitors were told that they were welcome to share a room with a group of passengers who had arrived by stagecoach. They were not impressed to be told that 'this was the best inn in the metropolis'.

The tired and disillusioned travellers took their leave and made their way to the Cross in search of a coffee-house where, they were assured, there was a woman who let accommodation. Courteously the pair were conducted to the sixth-floor landing of a tenement where the apartments were 'so infernal in appearance that you would have thought yourself in the regions of Erebus'. (Erebus is, in Greek mythology, the god of darkness and the intermediate region between earth and hades!) The accommodation was served by only two windows which looked out into a five-feet-wide passageway which was so dark that even on the brightest day the sun did not penetrate.

'It is extremely strange' reflected the Captain, 'that a city which is a thoroughfare into all Scotland and now little inferior in politeness to London in many respects, should not be better furnished with conveniences to strangers, or have a public lodging house where you can find tolerable entertainment'. But not all met with Topham's displeasure and he noted 'a thousand instances' of resemblances between Scotland and France. The air of mirth and vivacity, the quick and penetrating look, the spirit of gaiety which distinguished the French was equally visible in the Scots. And our visitor was impressed with the manners of local residents when they met strangers. They did not appear as if they had never seen each other before, or wished never to see each other again. They do not sit in sullen silence, looking at the ground, biting their nails and at a loss what to do with themselves, he observed:

> they appear to be satisfied with each other, or at least if they are really not so, they have the prudence to conceal their dislike. I never met with a more agreeable people, with more pleasing or more insinuating manners in my life.

Among the upper classes, small dinner parties were popular and it was considered an honour to be invited. The guests usually numbered about eight and the occasion was quite informal. It was noticed by our visitor, however, that women tended to consume more wine than their English counterparts but, as the Englishman tactfully explained 'the climate requires it'. The evening usually ended with a recital of Scottish songs.

Fashionwise Edinburgh ladies were not influenced by London, preferring the Paris fashions. These women, Captain Topham noted, dressed in general with more elegance and in a way better accommodated to their persons, size and shape than most of the European nations. Their complexion, too, was generally admired. The ladies used no make-up and Topham pointed out that 'neither their colour or complexion stand in need of it for I know not where they will find their equals in either'. Edinburgh men, according to our English visitor, had the worst tailors perhaps in the world.

The present Theatre [i.e. the Theatre Royal, which stood in Shakespeare Square, opposite Register House and opened in 1769 at a cost of £5000] Topham described as 'a plain structure'. Admission charges to the pit and boxes were three shillings. The pit was usually occupied by gentlemen who were not sufficiently dressed for the boxes. On busy nights however, ladies were also accommodated there, although the management very considerately provided a partition. Although the theatre had few ornaments it had an elegant appearance. The performances did not impress the southerner. Although murmurs of displeasure were heard from the audience 'they never rain down oranges, apples etc. on the heads of the unfortunate actors'. They were suffered quietly for an hour, and if they displeased they were literally heard no more'.

Whereas in England it was usual to drive the unfortunate actors from the stage, in Edinburgh the audience merely refrained from applauding. 'In such circumstances you discover the real manners of the people', observed Topham, who was suitably impressed with the behaviour of the town's residents.

The dances of Scotland he described as being entirely void of grace, and it was a mystery to him how Edinburgh women could sit quite unmoved at the-sprightly airs of an English country dance, but on hearing a Scottish air would move as if bitten by a tarantula. How was it, he questioned, that such a drowsy instrument as the bagpipes should be capable of inspiring such uncommon ardour? Dancing assemblies were fashionable modes of entertainment, and were conducted in an orderly manner. Those present were divided into sets and took their turn on the floor in strict rotation.

Oyster Cellars, described by Topham as 'high life below stairs', attracted both sexes of the upper classes. Invited to such an affair, one was ushered into a room where the guests were seated around a large table covered with dishes of oysters and pots of porter. Subsequently the tables were cleared, brandy punch was produced, and a jovial evening followed.

The women, it was noted, joined in the repartee to a much greater degree than would have been expected in England. Dancing formed a part of the evening's entertainment and at the end of a happy and enjoyable occasion, carriages were called. The cost of the evening had been two shillings for each guest.

Captain Edward Topham, who hailed from Yorkshire, educated at Eton and Trinity College, Cambridge, was a journalist who had travelled extensively on the Continent. He was therefore well qualified to make critical observations on conditions as he found them in Edinburgh. His residence of six months was sufficiently long to make a balanced judgement, and, apart from his initial experience in finding acceptable accommodation for the traveller, he was generally impressed with the Scottish capital. Above all, however, Topham's letters are extremely important; for they provide a valuable contribution to the social history of Edinburgh during the second half of the eighteenth century.

– 2 –
DR WILLIAM EDWARD PRITCHARD:
A DOUBLE MURDERER

You'll find the grave without any difficulty. Enter the Grange Cemetery by the east gate and walk straight ahead. It is only a short distance to where the tombstones are attached to the wall, ironically adjoining Lovers Loan, and it is the fifth one along.

The stone is showing signs of wear but it is still reasonably decipherable and reads:

> In memory of Michael Taylor who died 18th May 1867 aged 74 years, also of Jane his wife who died 25 Feby. 1865 aged 72 years, also their beloved daughter Mary Jane who died 18th March 1865 aged 38 years.

But what the memorial does not reveal are the bizarre circumstances surrounding the deaths of the two women, mother-in-law and wife of Dr Edward William Pritchard, who was later to stand trial for their murder by administering poison.

Michael Taylor was a successful Edinburgh silk and lace merchant and lived with his wife in respectable middle-class Lauder Road. They no doubt believed that their daughter Mary Jane had. made a good choice when she married the doctor and they gave him £500 towards establishing a medical practice in Glasgow.

Outwardly all was well and the marriage produced five children. But there was a seamier side to Pritchard. There were rumours of illicit affairs and financial debts. And there was a fire in which a young servant girl died.

The family moved house and 15-year-old Mary McLeod was employed as servant and children's nurse.

In late 1864 Mrs Pritchard began to suffer from bouts of sickness which were treated by her doctor husband. As a way of convalescing Mary Jane travelled to her parent's home in Lauder Road, Edinburgh, where, by all accounts, her health improved remarkably. She returned to Glasgow for Christmas and for a time she kept well. By January, however, the symptoms had returned, and gradually her condition deteriorated. It was therefore agreed

The grave at the Grange Cemetery, Edinburgh, where Mary Jane Pritchard and her mother, Jane Taylor, are buried. Both were poisoned by Dr Edward Pritchard.

that the elderly Mrs Taylor would come from Edinburgh to look after her daughter. In the meantime the symptoms persisted, and Mrs Pritchard was heard screaming with pain and demanding to see another doctor — Dr Gairdner. Such was her agitated state that the doctor did not consider it appropriate to examine the patient at that time. However, he returned next day and found Mrs Pritchard considerably improved — although he had his suspicions. Next day Mrs Taylor arrived to nurse her ailing daughter.

Mrs Pritchard's condition continued to improve and on one occasion she asked for tapioca — and then decided not to eat it. But her mother did and was violently sick. The poor innocent woman recovered and expressed the opinion that she must have had the same illness as her daughter!

Then on 25 February 1865, following a meal of sausages, Mrs Taylor died. She was examined by Dr Paterson, who was suspicious. Nevertheless, Mrs Taylor's body was taken to Edinburgh for burial in the Grange Cemetery, just a short distance from her home in Lauder Road. The cause of death was given as 'apoplexy'.

Meanwhile Mrs Pritchard's health continued to deteriorate. On the evening of 17 March she was found in a delirious state, demanding that attention be given to her mother, who was already dead. Dr Paterson was called. He prescribed a sedative, but by one o'clock in the morning she too was dead — exactly three weeks after her mother. Gastric fever was given as the cause of death, and her body was taken by train to be interred beside her mother at the Grange.

Suspicions were growing, however — two deaths in three weeks, mother and daughter, and this 'coupled with certain hints that had been received', resulted in intensive police investigations. While he was in Edinburgh arranging his wife's funeral, the police were granted a warrant for the arrest of Dr Pritchard. He was picked-up at Queen Street Station, Glasgow, as he alighted from the late-night Edinburgh train.

The Edinburgh authorities were informed and a post-mortem examination was carried out by Professor Douglas Maclaggan and Dr Henry Littlejohn, Edinburgh's Medical Officer of Health. Their findings revealed particles of antimony in Mrs Pritchard's liver. Her mother's body was exhumed on 31 March and again traces of antimony were found.

Shortly after 8 a.m. on 3 July 1865, Pritchard was brought from the Calton Jail to the High Court building. But it was not until 10.03 a.m. that the citizens of Edinburgh had their first sight of the accused. He was tall and stout with long thin hair and balding at the crown. He wore a mourning suit and hat. Dr Edward William Pritchard faced two charges of murder by poisoning his mother-in-law Jane Taylor and also his wife Mary Jane Pritchard.

The first witness was Catherine Lattimer who had worked as the family cook for ten years. She explained that she had gone to Carlisle for two weeks, and that Mrs Pritchard had been fine when she left. Asked how her mistress was when she returned, she replied, 'Not very well.' 'What was wrong with her?' 'She said she had a cold.' 'How long was she confined to bed?' — 'Four or five days.' 'Was she sick?' — 'Yes, at times.' 'Did any medical man attend her?' — 'Dr Gairdner was the first.' 'Did Mrs Pritchard tell you herself that she was sick?' — 'Yes.' 'Do you remember her going to Edinburgh to see her mother?' — 'Yes.' 'Did she appear to be quite well then?' — 'No, not quite well.' 'She returned a few days before Christmas'. 'How was she?' — 'A good deal better.' A week later her sickness returned. She was confined to bed three weeks later suffering from sickness, pain and cramp. Eventually Mrs Pritchard insisted on seeing another doctor and a servant was sent to ask Dr Gairdner to call.

Sixteen-year-old Mary McLeod, housemaid and children's nurse was asked if any doctor, other than her husband, attended Mrs Pritchard before she went to Edinburgh. 'No.' 'Did she get any medicine?' — 'Yes, a bottle; the contents were white like milk.' 'Anything else?' — 'Yes, red powders. Dr Pritchard gave the prescription.' 'Was Dr Pritchard beside her [his wife] when she died?' — 'Yes.' 'Was he weeping?' — 'Yes. He said, "Come back to your dear Edward."'

But the trial took a sensational turn when the witness, with extreme reluctance, was forced to admit that there had been a sexual relationship with the doctor; that she had been pregnant, and that the accused had administered a drug to procure an abortion. Damningly the witness was forced to admit that the doctor had promised to marry her should his wife die.

Professor William T. Gairdner of Glasgow University told the court that he had made two professional visits to Mrs Pritchard. He had been called by Dr Pritchard at the request of his wife. He said that he found Mrs Pritchard considerably exhausted and at the same time suffering from excitement caused by stimulants, and that he was very much puzzled by the symptoms.

Professor Gairdner had written to Mrs Pritchard's brother, Dr Taylor of Penrith (a former college friend), drawing his attention to his sister's illness. He admitted under cross-examination, however, that he did not indicate to Dr Taylor that he had suspected poisoning.

Apothecary John Campbell told the court that in November, December and February he had supplied the accused with strychnine, tartar emetic, laudanum and tartarised antimony.

Witness had been particularly struck by the large quantities of the latter drug bought by Pritchard. He had also bought a considerable amount of chloroform during the latter part of the previous year.

Dr Douglas Maclaggan, Professor of Medical Jurisprudence at Edinburgh University, said that the post-mortem examinations of both women had revealed large quantities of antimony — in his opinion the cause of death. Dr Henry Littlejohn, Edinburgh's Medical Officer of Health, confirmed the findings.

The court was told that Dr Pritchard's two bank accounts were over-drawn. Mr J.D. McBrair, trustee of Mrs Taylor's affairs, revealed that his client was in possession of trust funds of £3,000, of which £500 had gone to Dr Pritchard in June 1864, and by Mrs Taylor's will, Mrs Pritchard would have inherited £2,000.

In a declaration made before Sheriff Alison, Dr Pritchard said that he had been married for 15 years and had attended his wife in his capacity as family doctor. He was satisfied that Mrs Pritchard had died as a result of gastric fever. Pritchard claimed that he had administered no medicine, only champagne and brandy to support her strength. And six weeks before death, a little chloroform to induce sleep.

There were several uncomfortable minutes on the fourth day of the trial when the defence introduced two of the Pritchard children as witnesses. The first was Charles, aged eleven, who, because of his tender years, was not put on oath but was reminded by the judge that he must tell the truth.

'I am Dr Pritchard's eldest son. I lived with him in Glasgow. I was there when mamma died. My pappa and mamma lived happily together. Mamma and pappa were very fond of one another', he told the charged court.

And fourteen-year-old Jane said: 'I lived a good deal with my grandmother in Lauder Road. Papa was often there with my grandmother. Grandmother and pappa were fond of each other. I have often heard her speaking very kindly of him and him of her.'

The trial took a curious turn on the fifth day when questions were asked about Battley's Solution, today, a little-known concoction.

Thomas Fairgrieve, druggist, with a shop in Clerk Street, Edinburgh, confirmed that Mrs Taylor was one of his regular customers and that she habitually purchased Battley's Solution from his premises. Similar evidence was given by the representative of another Edinburgh firm. But what was the purpose of introducing questions on this mixture which was not even mentioned in the charges?

Battley's Solution was a mixture of opium, alcohol and water and was probably used as a painkiller. Unfortunately it could also be addictive, and Mrs Taylor used it in surprisingly large quantities. Was it possible that antimony or aconite could have contaminated the solution sold to Mrs Taylor, one of the expert witnesses was asked under cross-examination. This was not possible, the court was told. In other words, if traces of antimony had been found in Mrs Taylor's Batttley's, it had not been introduced at the time of preparation.

It took the jury only 55 minutes to reach their verdict of guilty. Dr Edward William Pritchard was told by the judge that he would be taken to Glasgow and there, on 28 July, he would suffer death by hanging.

There was one final, curious twist to the Pritchard case. On the day of the hanging, The *Weekly Scotsman* reported:

> This morning Dr Edward William Pritchard, the Glasgow poisoner, suffered the extreme penalty of the law for the murder by poison of his wife and mother-in-law at the common place of execution…The crimes for which this wretched man suffered punishment have not been equalled in their horrible atrocity since the case of Palmer.

Palmer? The case would have been fresh in the memories of many people, but today he is unknown. Dr William Palmer is believed to have poisoned his wife in 1854, his brother in 1855, and a friend later in the same year — all for financial gain. He was, however, convicted only of the murder of his friend, and was hanged at Stafford on 14 June 1856.

– 3 –
DID TWO LEITH MEN INVENT THE CHRISTMAS CARD?

Christmas is the season of Peace on Earth and Goodwill to all Men, and for days the postmen struggle through the snow, 'deep and crisp and even' (or more likely the slush), to deliver sackfuls of Christmas cards. But how many of the recipients ever give a thought to the origin of the card or realise that its beginnings may be traced to small premises in the old Kirkgate in Leith?

The Christmas card industry is a highly successful business, and the number of messages of greetings sent throughout the world during the festive season is incalculable. Yet, despite the popularity of the Christmas card, which has been with us for over 150 years, it has always been the subject of controversy: was it two Englishmen or two Leithers who were responsible for the production of the first Christmas card?

In 1843 an Englishman, Henry Cole, approached a friend, artist John Calcott Horsley, with a proposal: design a card which will convey a Christmas message, yet require nothing more that a signature. It was an idea which would be time-saving, doing away with the need for a laborious hand-written letter; but would this be in the true spirit of Christmas? History has proved that the answer is an emphatic 'Yes'. Needless to say, the introduction of the Christmas card in the south met with some opposition, mainly because the design consisted of a large affluent Victorian family toasting absent friends. In the eyes of the critics this was not in keeping with the Christian beliefs of Christmas and what it represented. Indeed, claimed the objectors, the card did nothing more than encourage the needless habit of consuming alcohol. It was ironic that such an accusation should be levelled against Horsley, the designer, whose morals were beyond reproach, and he was an active campaigner against the use of nude models by artists; his views allegedly earned him the title of 'Clothes-Horsley'! A card by William Maw Egley, with an intricate design showing various aspects of Christmas, was first thought to have been made in 1843; but it was later established that the year was 1848.

But was there a card produced in Leith two years previously? There is certainly strong evidence to suggest that in 1841 (two years before the English claim) Thomas Sturrock and Charles Drummond (he had a printing and publishing business at 133 Kirkgate) had produced a festive card. Much of the controversy surrounding their claim, however, is clouded by the reference to a New Year Card; not surprisingly, because of the leaning towards that day in Scotland.

From time to time the merits of the Leithers' case have been aired in the local press, but never more strongly than during a three-week period between 26 December 1934 and 14 January 1935. It was, however, a correspondence that was to shed a great deal of light on the background to the festive card.

The correspondence started quite innocently when, on 26 December 1934, the Port of Leith column in the *Edinburgh Evening News* remarked that at the festive time, when greetings were being exchanged through the medium of the card, it was appropriate to point out that the Christmas card is regarded as owing its origin to a Leith man, Thomas Sturrock. It was he who first suggested the New Year card, and in 1841 had supplied Charles Drummond with the design. Drummond had the sketch, a laughing face, with the motto 'Guid New Year and Mony o' Them' engraved on copper. The printed reproductions found a ready market. Two years later the English Christmas card made its first appearance, but by that time Sturrock's claim to be the originator of the festive card had been established in Edinburgh and London.

On Hogmanay the 'News' reported that a correspondent had drawn the paper's attention to a letter which had been contributed by him on 26 February 1907, shortly after Sturrock's tragic death in a car accident in Princes Street. This 1907 letter included the following:

> The card showed the curly head of a boy, open-mouthed (minus a tooth in the upper row) with fat, chubby cheeks, merry twinkling eyes and an expression of such hearty laughter that the happy combination, by the natural infectious process, produced the desired result on the onlooker, who was greeted with the wish of 'many happy years'. I am not aware whether the study was from life, but the whole expression is so vivid that it afterwards appeared as a plate in Vasey's *Philosophy of Laughter and Smiling*.
>
> The card was engraved by Mr A.T. Aikman of Edinburgh and was published by Mr Drummond, bookseller, Leith.

DID TWO LEITH MEN INVENT THE CHRISTMAS CARD?

The New Year was only five days old when James Telford wrote to the 'News' stating that the 'laughing face' referred to was originally engraved for Mr John Aikman, by his father, for use as a cover for a jest book. His grandfather, James Gould, who was employed at the time as an assistant in the Cross Post Office, 231 High Street, asked Alexander Aikman to engrave the words: 'A Happy New Year' and Many Happy Returns of the Season'. Hence, claimed Mr Telford, the first New Year card. To support his claim Mr Telford said that he had one of the first impressions from the plate.

Mr J.B. Aikman wrote that he was interested that James Telford also possessed one of the first New Year Cards dated (in pencil) 1853, two years before the one that had been reproduced in the 'News':

> As the engravings were made in the days of our grandfathers, about ninety years ago, I cannot say anything about Mr Telford's statement that the 'laughing face' was engraved by Mr Alexander Aikman for his son John, but as the latter was only eleven-years-old in 1841, it is possible that one of the faces might have been put on the cover of a jest book for the boy. It was always understood that Mr Sturrock was the originator of the card.

Douglas L. Sturrock told the 'News':

> I have read with interest the correspondence regarding the first New Year card, designed and invented by my grandfather, the late Thomas Sturrock. The copy which was in my grandfather's possession hung in the Leith Town Hall Chambers for many years and was returned to my late father on the amalgamation of Leith with Edinburgh. It is before me now and bears the inscription 'the first New Year's card, designed by Thomas Sturrock, printed by Charles Drummond, Leith, about 1841 or 42'.

At this point the correspondence on the origin of the Christmas card came to an end...for the time being.

The idea of sending Christmas cards was not an immediate success. For the first twenty years only a few firms and private individuals recognised the practice, but the industry made big advances during the 1870s when cards became more elaborate. It was about this time that single-page cards were replaced by the now traditional folded card and the familiar silk cord, or, more

WISHING YOU A MERRY CHRISTMAS AND A HAPPY NEW YEAR

Was this the first Christmas Card? (From an old print).

likely, ribbon. Gradually the Robin, Christmas tree, Santa Claus, mistletoe, holly and ivy found their places on the cards. Rarely were these cards used for propaganda purposes, but there were exceptions. During the Zulu Wars there were military cards, including one of a group of guardsmen headed by a drummer-boy, escorting a large Christmas pudding bedecked in flags. During the 1914–18 war, cards tended to be of a more sentimental theme, such as a single sprig of holly with the Union flag.

On the other hand the 1939–45 conflict leaned towards the amusing, perhaps as a psychological approach when, for a long spell, things were not looking too well for Britain and other free countries throughout the world. I still recall, as a youngster, receiving such a card from an uncle who was serving as a sergeant in the Royal Air Force in India.

DID TWO LEITH MEN INVENT THE CHRISTMAS CARD?

It showed an RAF sergeant (the stripes were attached to his arm with a piece of string) and he was floating through the air on a magic carpet dressed only in a loin cloth and wearing a turban. He was playing a flute, and from its mouth drifted the words, as popular today as they were during the late war years, 'I'm dreaming of a white Christmas'. This card came by airmail and I believe that before these greetings cards left India they were microfilmed and then enlarged in the United Kingdom prior to delivery.

The controversy surrounding the identity of the inventor of the Christmas card lay dormant for many years. The industry continued to expand and designs were changed frequently, to be more in keeping with current demand.

Then, just over 40 years ago an Edinburgh man, John Chalmers, contacted the *Evening Dispatch* and told the newspaper that he believed that he was in possession of a proof of one of the first Christmas cards published in 1841. Mr Chalmers said that he had obtained it in an unusual way. In 1946 his daughter had been working in a shop, and in the course of a conversation with an elderly gentleman had casually mentioned that her father was a printer. The customer left the shop but returned shortly afterwards, carrying a set of metal plates which he had obtained routinely in his scrap metal business. They were examined by the printer who suspected their historical significance and thought that they might be the original 1841 plates. Although corroded, the printer was able to clean them sufficiently to obtain reasonable prints before returning them to the owner. The reproduction showed a laughing face with a pair of extended hands and a display of fruit and wine. More interestingly, however, the open mouth revealed that an upper tooth was missing, a characteristic of the original Sturrock/ Drummond prints. But even more significantly it carried the message: 'Wishing you a Merry Christmas and a Happy New Year'.

Fifty years have elapsed since the story of the Sturrock/ Drummond plates came to light and, so far as I am aware, all traces of them have vanished. What does remain, however, is the controversy surrounding the invention of the Christmas card; and, as more than 150 years have elapsed since the introduction of the first festive card, the chances of solving the mystery diminish by the year.

– 4 –
SCOTLAND'S FORGOTTEN MEMORIAL

Strange, is it not, that in Edinburgh, the home of the world-famous Festival of Music and Drama, one of the least known memorials in the city is the one that commemorates the contribution made to music by three Scottish singers.

The Singers' Memorial is a plaque affixed to the rock on the right-hand side of the steps facing St Andrew's House. It bears the simple inscription 'In Memorium', and the wreathed profiles of John Wilson, John Templeton and David Kennedy — vocalists, who, in their day and generation, sang to packed audiences in various parts of the world. And those three men started their careers similarly, as precentors in Edinburgh churches.

John Wilson was born in the Canongate on Christmas Day, 1800. Apprenticed to a local printing firm, he subsequently joined the staff of James Ballantyne, printer of Sir Walter Scott's works. He developed an interest in music, and, after a spell singing in the choir at Duddingston Kirk, Wilson was offered and accepted the post as precentor at a city church.

At the age of 25, Wilson abandoned printing to study music. He made his first stage appearance at the Theatre Royal, Edinburgh, in *Guy Mannering*, and among those present on that memorable night was Sir Walter Scott. The Theatre Royal was located in Shakespeare Square and was demolished to make way for the large Post Office building at the east end of Princes Street and just a short distance from the Singers' Memorial.

The Canongate man's reputation as a tenor had risen considerably, and shortly afterwards he was invited to Covent Garden. Wilson moved to London, realising that his future lay there. During the following eight years his outstanding ability meant that he was capable of holding his own on the London stage. He then completed a highly successful trip to America. It was a proud John Wilson who, in 1842, received a Royal Command to sing before Queen Victoria at Taymouth Castle.

Seven years later, however, Wilson's life was to end suddenly and tragically. He was on a tour of North America performing his

Edinburgh's forgotten (and half-hidden) memorial, opposite St Andrew's House.

repertoire of Scots songs and attracting full houses. During a brief break in his hectic programme, he decided to relax with a spot of fishing. There he was soaked in an unexpected downpour, caught a chill, and shortly afterwards died of cholera, which had broken out in the area. John Wilson, who rose from humble beginnings in Edinburgh's Canongate, passed away on 8 July 1849, a comparatively young man.

John Templeton was born at Riccarton, near Kilmarnock, in 1802, and was a member of an extremely talented musical family. His father and brothers were renowned vocalists. Templeton arrived in Edinburgh at the age of twelve and served part of his singing 'apprenticeship' as a church precentor. His ability was beyond question, and it came as no surprise when he made it known that it was his intention to further his career in London. Templeton was well aware of the risks involved, but the Scot had confidence in himself.

Templeton moved cautiously, and his first appearance in the south was at Worthing, where it is said that he worked for three weeks without salary — a price he was prepared to pay in the interests of experience. He then moved to Brighton where he attracted sufficient attention to be offered a reasonably important engagement with the Southampton and Portsmouth Operatic Society. London was taking note, however, and Templeton was invited to Drury Lane.

As so often happens, Templeton's big chance came unexpectedly. The opportunity arose when the lead in *Don Giovanni* became available. There was only one week to go before the opening night, and the part was offered to the young Scot. He accepted without hesitation, and Templeton's performance was hailed by the critics as an outstanding success. Templeton never forgot his Scottish homeland. He travelled extensively and Scottish songs were always featured in his concerts. He retired when only 50-years old but was usually available for charity concerts.

He lived for 34 years after his 'retirement', remaining a much respected figure in the musical world. He died in London aged 84, and, it is said, left a fortune of £80,000.

The third member of the celebrated trio was David Kennedy, who was born in Perth on 15 April 1825. He too had music in his blood and both his father and his uncle were precentors at the North and South Kirks, Perth. David Kennedy's mother also played a big part in developing her son's talents, and it was she who took the young laddie to the harvest gatherings. There he learned the traditional versions of the farming community songs.

Kennedy was apprenticed to a house-painter which involved a fair amount of travel. On one occasion, while working about twelve miles from Perth, he decided that he would go to the town where Templeton was singing. But he had no money. It is said that he set out on a dark night in pouring rain and covered the distance in two hours. He listened from the doorway, made his way back and was ready for work at 6 a.m.

It has also been said. that Kennedy and his father walked from Perth to Edinburgh for a performance of Handel's *Messiah* in the Music Hall.

Kennedy moved to Edinburgh and in 1857 was appointed precentor at Nicolson Street United Presbyterian. Church. Competition for the post was fierce, for the salary was £40 per annum. David Kennedy was selected from 40 applicants and for five years he remained with this prosperous south-side congregation. His heart was set on public singing, however, and in 1859 he was invited to appear at the Burns' centenary celebration at the St George's Hall, Liverpool. Kennedy was a great success. Concerts at the Buccleuch Halls, Edinburgh, followed by a tour of Scotland, convinced him that he had the ability to make a full-time career on the stage. This he did, and was joined by his family.

After a successful series of concerts in Canada, the Kennedy family embarked on a world trip which included Australia, New Zealand, the United States and Canada. He died at Stratford, Ontario, 1886, while on a farewell visit. His body was brought home for burial in Edinburgh.

The last resting place of David Kennedy and members of his family is marked by an imposing memorial-stone which backs on to the wall at the south end of the Grange cemetery. The centre section reads:

> Here lies David Kennedy the Scottish singer. 'We'll meet and aye be fain in the land o' the leal'. Elizabeth Fraser his widow who died at Edinburgh 7 August 1897 aged 70 years.

On the right side are the following details:

> Also his son-in-law A.Y. Piasci, M.A. F.R.S.F who died at Edinburgh 9 Nov. 1890 aged 33 years.
> Also his daughter Marjory Kennedy-Fraser CBE Mus. Doc. died at Edinburgh 22 Nov. 1930 aged 73 years buried in Iona. Also of his daughter Jessie Kennedy wife of Tobias Matthay who died in Surrey 14 April 1937 aged 68 years. Also of his daughter Helen Kennedy wife of George Campbell who died at Halifax Nova Scotia 15 May 1941 aged 87 years. Also of his daughter Margaret Kennedy who died at Edinburgh 28 October 1951 aged 86.

And on the left, further details about the Kennedy family:

> In memory of his eldest son David who died at Maritzburg Natal 9 Dec. 1885 aged 35 years; also of his son James aged 26 years and his two daughters Kate aged 19 years and Lizzie aged 17 years who died at Nice 2; March 1881; also of his son Charles Kennedy M.D. who died at Edinburgh 17 May 1909 aged 50 years; Also of his son John H. Kennedy who died at Bristol 16 March 1912 aged 45 years; also of his son Robert Kennedy who died at Melbourne Australia 12 Sep. 1918 aged 66 years.

It was the London-based critic John Forbes-Robertson who said of Kennedy that he was 'by far the most perfect and dramatic exponent of Scots songs that Scotland has produced'. Despite his success Kennedy remembered the poor in Edinburgh and regularly gave concerts for their benefit. Oranges and buns were great favourites among the children! Although the Kennedy family enjoyed considerable success they also experienced tragedy. The year was 1881 and three of the Kennedy family; Kate, Lizzie and James, were on their way to study in Italy. They broke their journey at Nice where they attended a concert at the *Théatre des Italiens* on 23 March. Fire broke out during the performance and the trio perished.

Marjory Kennedy-Fraser

Gaelic music and song enjoy considerable popularity today, but how much of the material, now freely available, would have been lost but for the work of Marjory Kennedy-Fraser who spent a considerable part of her life ensuring its survival?

Marjory Kennedy was born into a musical family, being the daughter of David Kennedy, the third member of the famous trio of Scottish singers. By the age of twelve Marjory was already travelling with her father as his accompanist, and two years later she was to join the family on a world tour which lasted four years. Later Miss Kennedy studied singing at Milan and Paris. In 1887 she married A.Y. Fraser, the headmaster at Allan Glen's School in Glasgow, but sadly, a family which had experienced so much tragedy was struck once more when he died on 9 November 1890. A.Y. Fraser was only thirty-three years old.

The young widow then elected to settle in Edinburgh, where she devoted much of her time to teaching music and lecturing on musical subjects. Her interest in the music of the Gaels went back to before the turn of the century, but it was not until 1905 that she visited the Outer Hebrides. In her quest for material, Marjory Kennedy-Fraser undertook many arduous journeys. In one such trip, recorded in *A Life of Song*, she tells of leaving Edinburgh, on an August evening and sailing from Oban for Lochboisdale at six the following morning — then on to Eriskay in an open boat. At the time of her death it was reported that several of the Eriskay songs had been gathered at the evening ceilidh which was held at the post-office. Her *Songs of the Hebrides* was published in 1909 and *Sea Tangle* followed four years later. In between her busy 'collecting' schedule, Marjory Kennedy-Fraser found time to give

The flats at No. 6 Castle Street, where Marjory Kennedy-Fraser lived and died.

recitals with her sister, Margaret Kennedy, and her daughter, Patuffa Kennedy-Fraser. Her last recital, appropriately enough, was nationwide on the 'wireless'.

Marjory Kennedy-Fraser died at 6 Castle Street, Edinburgh, on 22 November 1930. She was 73-years old. In recognition of her services to music this remarkable lady had been granted a Civil List pension, was awarded the CBE and the University of Edinburgh recognised her achievements with a *Mus. Doc.* degree.

Three days after her death, a memorial service was held at St Giles' Cathedral. Very appropriately, as the huge congregation assembled, three pieces from *Songs of the Hebrides* were played, and later a lady member of the choir sang Marjory Kennedy-Fraser's *Land o' Heart's Desire*. The service was conducted by the

Very Revd Charles L. Warr, Dean of the Thistle, and minister of St Giles'. He told those present: 'She has done what no-one else has done, and which in fact, no one but herself could do…what the great Sir Walter did for lowland Scotland, what Neil Munro has done for those beyond the Highland line, Marjory Kennedy-Fraser effected for the immortal music of the Hebridean Isles.'

Contemporary newspaper reports state that Marjory Kennedy-Fraser was cremated at a private service held in the Edinburgh Crematorium, but her final resting place was to be Iona.

Fiddlers

Neil Gow is the name which immediately springs to mind whenever Scottish fiddlers are mentioned. He had a family of five — two daughters and three sons; the three males followed their father's career in music and became expert fiddlers. Nathaniel was the most successful, and he decided that he could best further his career in Edinburgh. During his early years in the Scottish capital he lived in Bailie Fyfe's Close in the High Street.

In 1796 Nathaniel Gow began selling music and musical instruments at 41 North Bridge, in partnership with William Shepherd. Business thrived, and such was the success of the venture that they moved to Princes Street and opened what is believed to have been the biggest shop of its kind in Scotland. Shepherd's death in 1812 was followed by a slump in turnover, and two years later Gow ceased trading.

By 1818 Gow was again retailing, this time in partnership with his son Neil. They opened in Princes Street, and five years later moved to Hanover Street. Shortly afterwards his son died. Nathaniel Gow was determined to carry on, however, and once more was back in Princes Street, this time in a joint venture with Murray Galbraith. After only eight months, however, Gow was declared bankrupt and the property at his home in Hanover Street was sold to help satisfy his creditors.

In 1791 Nathaniel Gow took over from his brother as leader of the musicians who performed at the Assembly Balls. These talented men were considered to be the finest in the country, and in 1822, when George IV was at Dalkeith Palace, they were invited to provide the music. Gow was also a successful teacher, and this work included a weekly lesson at Dalkeith Palace for which he received a fee of two guineas plus travelling expenses.

Nevertheless, he was dogged by debt. He died on 19 January 1831, and is believed to have been buried beside his son at Greyfriars, although I can find no stone.

James McIntosh was another Highlander who headed for Edinburgh. He was born at Inver on 11 December 1791, and was the last pupil of the celebrated Neil Gow. McIntosh was taught on an instrument supplied by Nathaniel Gow. In the city McIntosh was apprenticed as a joiner while he pursued his musical career at the town assemblies. Such was his ability that McIntosh was among those who played at that historic ball held at Dalkeith Palace in 1822. McIntosh died at Edinburgh in 1877 and was buried in Dalry cemetery.

Pate Bailie was described as one of the finest untutored fiddlers to be born in Scotland and was possibly second to Neil Gow. Details of his birth are vague, but he is believed to have been born at Liberton about 1774. His early working life was spent at the Burdiehouse lime quarries and later he was employed as a stonemason. In this capacity he reportedly broke a leg while carrying out work at the University of Edinburgh.

Once he had made his mark as a fiddler, however, music became his life. He was patronised by the nobility, and was a regular visitor to Dalkeith Palace. A story is told that Bailie, while travelling from Leith to Burntisland, having been invited to play at a great county ball in the 'Kingdom', was challenged by a fellow-traveller to play 'The East Neuk of Fife' with the ten variations. He complied and added ten of his own before the journey was completed.

Pate, however, had one great temptation — whisky; but it made no difference to his playing for he could fiddle a reel lying flat on his back just as well as he could standing on his two feet!

Fiddle Makers

In the early years of the eighteenth century Matthew Hardie of Edinburgh was well known not only as a fine fiddle maker but also for his 'school' which produced many notable craftsmen. His work earned him the title 'the Scottish Stradivari'. He was born in 1755 and carried out business in Calton Road, close to where it is now crossed by the Regent Bridge. The dingy premises, consisting of a front and back shop, served also as a school for his pupils. And how much mythology is attached to the story of how Hardie, while walking in the vicinity of Cramond, picked up a piece of wood. He allegedly struck it with a stone in order to test the tone and remarked on its suitability as a fiddle breast. Hardie continued his journey with the wood tucked under his arm and shortly afterwards called at a farmhouse for a drink of milk. While in the kitchen Hardie spotted a maple-wood baking board which he easily acquired by offering a new one in return. In due course the two pieces of wood found their way into the workshop where they were turned into what has been described as being as fine an instrument as was ever made by that craftsman.

The import of cheap German factory-made instruments seriously affected Hardie's business, and it is believed that he spent a period of time in the debtors' prison. But while in confinement he continued to produce fiddles. In old age he was admitted to St Cuthbert's Poorhouse which was located near the foot of Lothian Road, where the former 'Caley' railway station stood. There he died in 1826 and was buried at Greyfriars Churchyard.

His son Thomas inherited the business, and although he was a capable worker, he lacked the fine qualities of his father. Less and less money came into the shop and finally Thomas Hardie was forced to move into even smaller premises which were located behind Shakespeare Square, and to the rear of the Theatre Royal. By this time, however, Tom Hardie had become addicted to drink. He was befriended by William Yoole of St Andrews, who had received some tuition from Hardie senior. In an attempt to rehabilitate the son, he invited him to the Fife town, but all in vain.

Tom Hardie made his way back to Edinburgh and for a period he was living at 97 High Street, adjacent to 'Heave Awa' Close'. His drinking became worse, and he was believed to be living in poverty in the vicinity of Castlehill/Lawnmarket. He died in 1858 from injuries sustained when he fell down stairs while in a drunken state. Thomas was buried beside his father in Greyfriars.

Yet another Hardie — James — was in business as a fiddle maker in Edinburgh between 1830 and 1855, but he was not related to the other Hardies. He was by profession a pattern-maker, and this training undoubtedly helped him to success in the musical sphere. James Hardie's premises were located in a house situated between Arthur Street and Salisbury Street in the Pleasance, and his work was of a high order.

The name Alexander Howland Smith will be familiar to readers of *Edinburgh Curiosities*, published by John Donald Publishers Ltd in 1996. Smith was the clerk who fooled the experts and flooded the market with countless numbers of literary and historical documents. The law finally caught up with him and in 1893 he was found guilty at the High Court, Edinburgh, of fabricating documents. He was sentenced to twelve months, imprisonment which he served in Calton Jail.

At the time of his arrest in 1892, Alexander Howland Smith's age was given as 33 years, which means that he was born in 1859. I was therefore greatly surprised when consulting a directory of Scottish fiddle makers to find the following entry:

Alexander Howland Smith, Edinburgh, was born in Edinburgh in March, 1859, and is now living . He has made about thirty violins and four violincellos on the models of Stradivari and Joseph Guarneri. These are covered with amber oil varnish of a reddish-yellow colour. Labels, printed from types on rough white paper, with the date handwritten: 'Alexander Howland Smith, Edinensis, hoc fecit, 1897'.

Was it just coincidence and that there were two men, both born in 1895, with the unusual middle name of Howland, or did the crafty Alexander Howland 'Antique' Smith have another string to his bow?

Edinburgh Musical Festivals

When did the first Edinburgh Musical Festival take place...1947 perhaps? Well, not quite. In fact you will have to go back to the early part of the 19th century to find the answer; over a period of nine years a group of enterprising men got together and organised three highly successful and profitable festivals. They were not subsidised by public money and in fact they showed a profit which went to the welfare of the poor in the town.

The first, described as 'a Grand Musical Festival, opened on Tuesday 31 October 1815, and continued for the remainder of the week. Morning performances were held in Parliament Hall and in the evening audiences flocked to Corri's Rooms which stood at the junction of Broughton Street and Little King Street. Patrons could purchase six tickets for three guineas and they were transferable. In return, ticket-holders were able to enjoy works by Mozart, Handel, Beethoven, Hyden and others. The capital was crowded with visitors and the performances were well attended

The plaque at No. 84 Great King Street, where Felix Yaniewicz lived.

by what was described as 'the largest assemblages of beauty and fashion ever seen in the city'. It was a highly organised occasion and the directors included a certain Mr Walter Scott, Henry Mackenzie (*The Man of Feeling*), Sir William Fettes, the Hon. Henry Erskine, Principal Baird, Gilbert Innes of Stow and Lord Grey. The venture was a resounding success, not least financially, and £1,500 was distributed to charity.

There was a second festival in 1819 which attracted 8,526 theatre-goers for the six performances. Receipts were £5,256 and expenses amounted to £4,024, leaving over £1,200 for distribution among Edinburgh's needy. This was a drop of £300 on the previous festival and the writing was already on the wall.

The third and last of these 19th-century events was held in 1824, with morning performances in Parliament House and at the theatre in the evening. Interestingly the cost of the tickets remained at three guineas. Although the performances were again well attended and receipts came to £,4,940, expenditure was again up. The profit at the end of the week had dropped to only £543. And the reason? — 'High demand of the principal singers'. The organisers decided that they could not justify further events.

But as a result of these festivals the Edinburgh Institution for the Encouragement of Sacred Music was born. An appeal for choristers attracted 780 hopefuls. About half were chosen.

And where can you find a permanent reminder of Edinburgh's first musical festival? At the entrance to number 84 Great King Street. There, cut into the stone is the inscription: 'Felix Yaniewicz, Polish composer and musician, co-founder of First Edinburgh Festival, lived and died here, 1823–1848.

– 5 –
CHARLOTTE SQUARE:
ITS HISTORY AND RESIDENTS

The Edinburgh citizens who deserted the cramped, dirty, insanitary conditions of the Old Town and crossed the North Bridge to take up residence in the fine streets to the north, could not have failed to be impressed. There they found broad streets, a fine example of forward-planning, to meet the traffic needs into the twentieth century, and ample open space. Charlotte Square is a fine example of what these 18th-century developers had in mind.

With St Andrew Square at the east end of George Street (named after George III), St George's Square was considered to be an appropriate address for the dwellings to be erected in the square at the western extremity; but it was too late. George Square was already laid out and so Charlotte Square was adopted — an acknowledgement to the wife of George III.

Robert Adam completed his plans for the square in 1791, but he did not live to see his masterpiece completed. He died in March of the following year, at the age of 64 and was buried at Westminster. At the time of his death it is believed that Adam was actively engaged in eight public works and 25 private buildings.

The bulk of the former church on the west side of Charlotte Square tends to catch the eye, but very quickly the attention turns to the north side — a lasting memorial to the Kirkcaldy-born genius. He was paid £200 for the layout plan for the square and five guineas for each house he designed in detail. The feuing conditions required that the houses to be built on the north side should be constructed 'on a regular plan to conform to an elevation by the late Mr Robert Adam, Architect, and the ornamental parts of the fronts to be finished in the manner there-in set furth'.

Residents

Charlotte Square immediately became a prestigious address and over the years provided homes for some of the town's wealthiest families. In 1806, Sir John Sinclair of Ulbster occupied number 6. Sinclair was educated at Edinburgh, Glasgow and Oxford

Sir John Sinclair. From Kay's Original Portraits.

universities and he qualified as a lawyer. While in the south of England he met Sarah, daughter of Alexander Maitland, who was of Scottish descent. The young Scot proposed and was accepted, but a hitch developed — his future mother-in-law! This lady, reluctant to lose her daughter, insisted on a promise from Sinclair that he would live permanently in England. This ultimatum he could not meet, and he set off for a continental holiday, believing that the marriage would not take place. He returned to learn that Sarah had prevailed upon her mother and that the wedding could now go ahead. Following their marriage on 26 March 1776, the couple departed to live in Thurso! In 1780 Sinclair was elected Member of Parliament for Caithness. He lost the seat in 1784 but was later returned for Lostwithiel in Cornwall. Sarah died in 1785, leaving two young daughters. The following year Sinclair was created a baron; and three years after the death of his wife he remarried. His bride was the Honourable Diana, the only daughter of Lord Macdonald. Soon afterwards they settled in Edinburgh, first in the Canongate, before moving to 6 Charlotte Square, and subsequently George Street. It is said that as a form of exercise he regularly walked to Leith. In 1791 Sinclair embarked on the compilation of *The Statistical Account of Scotland*, a task which took between seven and eight years, and consisted of 21 volumes. Sinclair was a great supporter of the celebrated writer Malachi Malagrowther — Who? Malachi Malagrowther was the *nom-de-plume* used by Sir Walter Scott in 1826, when the Government proposed to limit the issue of banknotes. This would have had a serious effect in Scotland, and Scott, under his *nom-de-plume*, expressed his views on the matter with a number of letters which were published in the *Edinburgh Weekly Journal*.

Sinclair was an internationally known figure and, among many others, he corresponded with George Washington, John Adams and Thomas Jefferson, the first three Presidents of the USA. Any person of note who visited Scotland would almost certainly have carried a letter of introduction to John Sinclair. He died at his George Street home in December 1835, and according to the 19th-century writer James Paterson 'was buried on the 30th in the Royal Chapel of Holyrood'.

There were thirteen children from Sinclair's two marriages but without doubt it is to his daughter Catherine that Edinburgh is most indebted.

Catherine Sinclair was born into a well-to-do family, and she could have spent her time, as so many of her class did, enjoying a life of leisure But this public-spirited woman chose to devote her life to caring for the less fortunate citizens of Edinburgh. It was Catherine Sinclair, an author with 37 titles to her credit, who introduced public seats to the busy streets of Edinburgh, a feature which remains popular to this day. She founded and financed the Volunteer Brigade for the boys of Leith; opened a school where girls from working class homes were taught domestic work, and provided shelters where cabmen could relax while waiting for 'fares'.

Cooking centres were also provided by this great benefactress. The first, opened at 60 Queensferry Street, proved to be so popular that a second followed shortly afterwards at 33 George IV Bridge. These premises consisted of a kitchen with separate dining rooms

The Catherine Sinclair Memorial.

for students and families. For as little as 4½p it was possible to obtain a meal consisting of soup, meat, potatoes and bread.

But nothing perpetuated the name of Catherine Sinclair more than her much appreciated drinking fountain, which stood at the junction of Lothian Road and Princes Street. The Sinclair Fountain was presented to the city in 1859 and is notable for being the first drinking fountain in Edinburgh. For fourteen years it was a popular amenity where the thirst of man and beast alike could be slaked on warm summer days. But it was a facility which could be put to other uses. In those far off days of the horse-drawn tram, when public houses were open all day, many of our policemen were from the north and were not averse to a drop of whisky. Working on points duty at the West End, it was no easy matter for the 'bobby' to get a drop of the 'cratur' without being seen, but there was a way of overcoming this problem: a signal was passed to the local newsvendor who obligingly ran to the nearest public house to purchase a gill which, at that time, cost between six and seven pence. The vendor then went to the well, emptied the whisky into one of the chained cups and signalled to the constable. He sauntered over and drank with pleasure.

Alas, on 4 June 1873, on the casting vote of Lord Provost James Cowan, it was decided that, because of the increase in traffic, the fountain was causing congestion and would have to be removed. There was an immediate outcry. Letters appeared in the newspapers, and all but one opposed the Council's decision. It was pointed out that this was the only fountain in the area, and a survey carried out only a short time previously established that during a three-hour spell 273 horses had been watered at the well; proof surely that it should be retained.

The controversy was by no means a local dispute. There was a letter from a correspondent in Tunbridge Wells, part of which read:

> I have just seen — with more sorrow than I can well express — in a late number of your paper, that the Sinclair Fountain, which held its ground successfully through so many onslaughts, has at last been a victim to that great juggernaut the tramway. Forbid it, shade of kind Miss Sinclair. Forbid it in all humanity...

The writer went on to explain that for many years he had driven past the fountain four times a day and had derived much pleasure from watching the horses drinking at it. Never once had he witnessed them causing any delay. He enclosed £10 towards a fund to fight the Council decision.

There was one citizen who supported the Council's views, but he chose to hide under the *nom-de-plume* 'Civus'. This writer pointed out that no correspondent seemed to be aware that a pillar well was placed at each cab stance in the city and that a pail was provided in order that the horses might also drink. They were never used, he claimed, and he went on to accuse the cabmen of adjourning to nearby public-houses 'for something stronger than water', leaving one boy to attend to the horses, hence the reason for it being necessary to use the fountain. It was evident that 'Civus' was set on having the fountain removed, for he concluded:

> I have seen all the principal towns in the Empire, as well as those of Rome, Naples and many other of the chief towns of the Continent, but never in my experience, either as a professional man or a citizen

of the world, have I seen anything to compare with, in utter contemptibility, with the ugliness of the Sinclair Fountain, and this aggravated one hundredfold from the fact it occupies a site, the finest in the city and in a street whose beauty cannot be matched.

The campaign for its retention was successful, however, for at a meeting of the Town Council on 26 June the decision to remove the fountain was reversed. For over seventy years this landmark remained on its familiar site, but on 2 February 1932, the matter was again raised at a Council meeting.

Once more the decision was taken to remove the fountain, but this time the council officials acted swiftly, and less than two weeks later the work of dismantling had been completed. Curiously, about the same time the City Architect and Burgh Engineer had reported that the fountain was in need of repair and the cost was estimated at £390.

There was a general belief among Edinburgh's citizens that every effort would be made to find an alternative site. But two years on, with no evidence of any progress, a newspaper reporter began to ask questions. He eventually traced the fountain in the Burgh Engineer's yard in the Cowgate. Requests for information about the re-siting of the well were met with silence. The fight went on, and in 1935 there was some hope when it was suggested that a permanent location might be found near the bandstand in West Princes Street gardens. No further action was taken. Not even the war years allowed the subject of this now famous fountain to be forgotten, and, in 1941, the newspaper again reminded the council of their promise to relocate this former prominent city landmark. This time the local authority had a ready-made answer, and a spokesman was quick to point out that no action could be taken for the duration of the war. To strengthen this argument he went on to explain that other cities, far from replacing structures, were removing public monuments to places of safety. In 1950 an observant citizen noted that a tram island now occupied the site; surely space could be found to reinstate Catherine Sinclair's gift to the town. This plea was also met with indifference.

The years passed, and then in 1964 I decided to investigate. With reluctance a council official suggested that the fountain 'might' be in the yard at Russell Road. It was, stacked neatly in a corner. Unfortunately, more than thirty years had elapsed since the council's controversial act; most of the councillors and officials

The Catherine Sinclair Drinking Fountain, reminding humans that 'water is not for man alone'.

involved in the decision were no longer in the Chambers and there was little enthusiasm to raise the embarrassing subject. At some point over the ensuing years, this once-familiar piece of street furniture which had been appreciated by man and animal alike, was removed from Russell Road, its whereabouts unknown; it was rediscovered quite by chance.

The council premises at Stanwell Street were known to hold a number of ornamental stones which had been accumulated over the years, and a decision was taken to identify the stones and compile an inventory. In the course of this work a stone was discovered bearing the inscriptions:

WATER IS NOT FOR MAN ALONE: A BLESSING (UP)ON THE GIVER: and DRINK AND BE THANKFUL.

Enough to identify the missing Catherine Sinclair drinking fountain.

More than sixty years have passed since the well was removed, and it has had several 'homes', but once more what has survived is again on public display and can be seen on the cycleway/walkway beside Gosford Place, Leith. It was placed there in 1983, at the section named Steadfastgate, to mark the centenary of the Boys' Brigade.

Catherine Sinclair died suddenly, aged sixty-four, at the Vicarage, Kensington, the home of her brother. She had been ill for two months. In acknowledgement of her work for Edinburgh's needy families, a fine statue was erected at the corner of North Charlotte Street and St Colme Street. Included in the inscription cut into the stone are the words:

SHE WAS A FRIEND OF ALL CHILDREN AND THROUGH HER BOOK 'HOLIDAY HOUSE' SPEAKS TO THEM STILL.

Catherine Sinclair lived at 133 George Street and despite her considerable philanthropic work which must have occupied a considerable amount of her time, she was also a prolific writer. The sales of her book *Beatrice* are believed to have exceeded 100,000 copies within a few months of publication. The Sinclair family were renowned for their height and the pavement outside their residence was known as 'The Giants' Causeway'.

Number 9 might well be known as the doctors' house for here resided two distinguished medical men, James Syme and the future Lord Lister of antiseptics fame. Syme was educated at Edinburgh's High School and later at the University of Edinburgh. He was appointed Professor of Surgery at Edinburgh in 1833 and was recognised as the greatest living authority in his speciality. Syme had one achievement outwith medicine to his credit when, in 1818, he revealed a method of making waterproofing. He died in 1870. Joseph Lister arrived in the city in 1853 to spend a month on postgraduate study with the celebrated Syme. He remained until 1860 (having married Professor Syme's daughter Agnes in 1856) when he was appointed Professor of Surgery at Glasgow. Lister returned to Edinburgh in 1869 to succeed his father-in-law in the Chair of Clinical Surgery and took up residence at number nine.

A few doors away at No. 12 lived Sir John Marjoribanks, when Mr Walter Scott, advocate, was granted the Freedom of Edinburgh (with a piece of plate, value 50 guineas) and 'whose celebrity as a writer has contributed so much to raise the fame of his native country'. The date was 22 December 1813. It was during the provost-ship of Marjoribanks that the Regent Bridge and Calton Jail projects went ahead. Next door, No. 13, was for many years the home of Sir William Fettes, probably Edinburgh's best-known early 19th-century Lord Provost, remembered as the benefactor who financed the building of the world-famous college which bears his name. Fettes was born on 25 June 1750, and was educated at the High School. In an 18th-century directory there is an entry: 'William Fettes, grocer, head of Bailie Fyfe's Close; house 57 Princes Street'. He was twice elected Lord Provost (1800–02 and 1804–06). And one important duty he fulfilled was to serve on the jury at the trial of Deacon Brodie in 1788. Both were businessmen; they must have known each other; nevertheless, Brodie went to the gallows. Justice had to be done and seen to be done.

Fettes married Maria Malcolm, daughter of Dr John Malcolm of Ayr, in March 1787. They had only one child, a son, also named William, who was admitted to the Faculty of Advocates in 1810, but died in Berlin five years later.

William Fettes senior was a very successful businessman and accumulated a large fortune. He retired from business in 1800 and devoted the remainder of his time to administering his various estates. In 1804 he was honoured with a baronetcy. Sir William died on 27 May 1836 — only twenty days after the death of his wife — and was buried in the Canongate graveyard close to where his father had been interred. The inscription on the memorial reads:

> Sacred to the Memory of Sir William Fettes of Comely Bank, Baronet, Lord Provost of the City of Edinburgh in 1801 and 1802; and a second time in 1805 and 1806. Born 25th. June 1750, died 27th. May 1836. Also of Maria Malcolm his wife, who died 7th. May 1836; and Willam Fettes advocate, their only son, who died at Berlin, 13th. June 1815, aged 27 years.
>
> _____
>
> Over the grave of its Founder the Trustees of the Fettes Endowment have erected this Monument in grateful recognition of the enlightened benevolence which devoted the acquisitions of an honourable life to the useful purpose of providing for the children of his less-fortunate fellow countrymen the blessings of a sound and liberal education.

The Earl Haig Statue on the Castle esplanade.

In fact Fettes left the considerable sum of £166,000 for the provision of the college which was constructed between 1864–70.

Lord Cockburn, judge and writer of the famous *Memorials*, occupied, No. 14, and is remembered for the great interest he had in the preservation of Edinburgh. No fewer than three people of note occupied No. 17 at one time or another, among them James Wolfe Murray who appeared for the prosecution at the trial of Deacon Brodie; he later became a judge. Wolfe Murray was the householder in 1811. Nineteen years later the Rt Hon David Boyle, Lord Justice General, was resident. And here, in 1856, was born the future Viscount Haldane. Educated at the Edinburgh Academy and at the University of Edinburgh, he was liberal MP for East Lothian (1885–1911), Lord Chancellor (1912–15), and was closely involved in restructuring the army. He died in 1928.

Dr Elsie Maud Inglis of the Elsie Inglis Maternity Hospital fame, obtained part of her education in a small school located at No. 23. This lady, whose services were declined by the War Office during the 1914–18 campaign, worked tirelessly for the Serbs and died in 1917. Elsie Inglis was born in India in 1864 and studied at Edinburgh, Glasgow and Dublin. She was surgeon at Bruntsfield Hospital, established a hospice at 219 High Street, and between 1898 and 1914 practised medicine at 8 Walker Street. By a strange coincidence, at 24 Charlotte Square, was born on 19 June 1861, Douglas, Earl Haig, Commander-in-Chief during the First World War.

St George's Church (West Register House)

Robert Adam did design a church for Charlotte Square but it was never constructed, probably because of cost. The task was given to Robert Reid. His revised design did not meet with general approval, and, as one 19th-century critic wrote:

> Had the civic authorities adhered as closely to the designs of Mr Adam in the erection of St George's Church, as in the other buildings of the Square, they would not, from a mistaken notion of economy, have erected an edifice, which, although it may be considered by a superficial observer as highly ornamental to the place where it is situated, is, when minutely and critically examined, found to be destitute of all architectural proportions, and an object of general disapprobation.

On Tuesday 14 May 1811, Lord Provost William Calder, Magistrates and Town Councillors met in St Andrew's Church, George Street, at 2 p.m. and walked to the west side of the square where the foundation stone of St George's church was laid by the Lord Provost. This is an historic date in local government history, for, immediately after the stone-laying ceremony, the Lord Provost and councillors again lined up and made their way in procession to the High Street and formally took over the Royal Exchange (built 1753–61) as the City Chambers.

The church was three years in construction and served this wealthy congregation for 147 years. In 1959 dry rot was discovered and an appeal for funds was successful, but other faults were found and the cost of repair proved to be very substantial. Sadly, in 1961, the church closed, and for some time the future of the building was in doubt. At the same time Register House was facing storage problems, and in 1964 the decision was taken to convert St George's Church into West Register Rouse as a repository for public records. Work began in 1968 and West Register House was opened by the then Secretary of State for Scotland on 2 April 1971. A sum of £450,000 had been spent — but the former St George's Church had been saved.

Andrew Thomson, the first minister at St George's, died suddenly on 9 February 1831, but he is remembered to this day as the composer of the tune 'St George's Edinburgh' ('Ye Gates, lift up your heads').

The Albert Memorial

Did Queen Victoria unveil the Albert Memorial in Charlotte Square? It is a question that is often asked, and the answer is that the circumstances are open to interpretation although the Queen was present at that memorable and moving occasion. Prince Albert died on Saturday 14 December 1861, and most Edinburgh citizens heard the news from church pulpits the following morning. It was received with shock; Prince Albert was only 42 years old and had been in Edinburgh less than three months previously, when he had laid the foundation stones at the post office, and at the museum in Chamber Street.

Edinburgh took the initiative, and, in February 1862, it was suggested that a national monument should be erected in memory of the late Consort. But before long it was evident that Glasgow, Aberdeen, Dundee and Perth were not in favour of this proposal. The capital, in conjunction with the other areas of Scotland (but excluding these cities) launched an appeal which realised £13,400. Subsequently competitive designs were invited, and it was announced that £12,000 would be available for this purpose. The Queen was consulted with regard to design and location, and she nominated a Committee of Advice, which consisted of the Duke of Buccleuch, Lord Provost Charles Lawson, Sir William Gibson-Craig, Sir John McNeill KCB, Dr Lyon Playfair (Professor of Chemistry, Edinburgh, 1858–69), MP for Universities of Edinburgh and St Andrews 1868–85; Post-Master-General 1873 and first Baron Playfair), and Sir George Harvey, President of the Royal Scottish Academy. Not surprisingly this prestigious work attracted the country's top artists. A short-list of six was drawn-up and submitted

The Prince Albert Memorial with West Register House in the background.

to Queen Victoria for her approval. She in turn consulted Sir Charles Eastlake, President of the Royal Academy, but without indicating her preference. The two were in agreement and their choice was one of three submitted by Edinburgh-based John Steell showing the prince in the uniform of a Field-Marshal and mounted on a horse. Steell's other proposals were a drawing of a pedestrian Prince Albert in the act of contemplating a globe, and the other, intended for a site on Arthur's Seat, was a clay equestrian model of the Consort on the summit of an arched Gothic structure, intended to be viewed from a distance. The 32-feet chosen design was completed as submitted with only a few minor alterations. At the request of Steell, sculptors William Brodie RSA, Clark Stanton RSA and George McCallum were invited to carry out some of the work, although Steell undertook the equestrian statue and base reliefs. He was in overall charge of the commission. McCallum died at an early stage in the work and D.W. Stevenson joined the team.

The Albert Memorial was unveiled on 17 August 1876 (15 years after the death of the Prince) in the presence of Queen Victoria, Prince Leopold and Princess Beatrice, on a site 'which was loyally offered by the proprietors of Charlotte Square'. Just before 4 p.m.

the Queen took her place on the dais. During the ceremony, and in a touching moment, music composed by Albert was played by the 79th Highlanders, the Camerons.

In welcoming the Queen to Edinburgh, the Duke of Buccleuch said:

> The Executive Committee for the erection of the Scottish National Memorial to His Royal Highness the Prince Consort have today the high honour and gratification of presenting that memorial in its completed form to your Majesty and to the people of Scotland.
>
> The subscribers to the memorial numbered very many thousands of your Majesty's Scottish subjects. Contributions were received from every county and nearly every parish in Scotland. All classes of society from the highest and the wealthiest, to the lowliest and poorest, willingly combined, according to their respective ability, to render this memorial a monument worthy of the occasion...
>
> It is an auspicious coincidence that this day the 17th. August is the anniversary of the birth of Her Royal Highness the Duchess of Kent, your Majesty's beloved mother. The memory of Her Royal Highness will ever be revered by the people of this country for the conspicuous virtues of Her Royal Highness' life and especially for her admirable nurture of their future sovereign. The Executive Committee humbly request your Majesty to be graciously pleased to unveil the memorial in the sight of the present assemblage.

In reply the Queen said:

> I receive with pleasure your loyal address. I am well aware of the feeling in Scotland which prompted the raising of this National memorial and assure you that I heartily appreciate the affection and admiration manifested in this country for my dear husband, as well as the loyalty and attachment to me which has ever been the character of my Scottish subjects. I thank you heartily for the kind allusion you have made to my beloved mother on this day the anniversary of her birth. Her frequent residence in this your city and its neighbourhood proved how much she loved the Scottish nation.

And Victoria's part in the unveiling ceremony? At the conclusion of the Queen's reply the Rt Hon R.A. Cross, the Secretary of State, after exchanging a few words with the Queen said: 'I have much pleasure in saying, by Her Majesty's command, that it is her desire the statue be now unveiled'.

Within seconds the canvas which covered the statue and the wrappings of the pedestal were removed to reveal the statue to the gaze of the general public. Thereafter the four sculptors were introduced to the Queen. Only then did Victoria leave the dais and accompanied by the principal sculptor, members of the royal family and officials, spent some time admiring the statue.

Throughout the ceremony Queen Victoria appeared to be completely relaxed, but what were her thoughts? She surely recalled Albert's last visit to Edinburgh when, on 23 September 1861, he had laid the foundation stones at the General Post Office (which she passed on her way to the unveiling ceremony in Charlotte Square) and the museum at Chambers Street — possibly the last public engagements he carried out. It was an overcast day with an unusually cold and biting wind blowing. Victoria had remained at Holyrood, but Albert had been subjected to two very long ceremonies which included prayers and therefore a need to remain bareheaded. Less than three months later Victoria's beloved Albert was dead.

At the conclusion of the ceremony in the late afternoon, Victoria returned to Holyrood and immediately John Steell and Professor Oakeley arrived at the palace by royal command, where the Queen, having first ascertained the first names of the sculptor and musician, honoured both men with knighthoods. Within an hour of returning to Holyrood, Victoria, accompanied by Prince Leopold and Princess Beatrice, left the royal residence and drove through the park by way of St Margaret's Loch and Dunsappie; on reaching St Leonard's gate the coach went by way of Dalkeith Road and on to visit the historic Craigmillar Castle. The royal party returned to the palace through Duddingston. And there was one final piece of good news for the city during that memorable royal visit, for it was announced that Queen Victoria was to bestow a knighthood on Lord Provost James Falshaw.

Sir James Falshaw has a unique distinction: he is believed to be the only Englishman who has been elected Lord Provost of the City of Edinburgh. His family hailed originally from the Yorkshire Dales, but he was born and educated in Leeds. Falshaw qualified as a civil engineer, a fortunate choice of career, for this was a period when engineers were in great demand for railway construction. He came to Scotland in 1845, initially to Nairn, where he served on the council, and in 1858, he took up residence in Edinburgh. The Yorkshireman retained his keen interest in local government, and two years later he stood for election in the city but was defeated. In 1861, however, he was elected and served for 16 years. With his engineering qualification, Falshaw was an invaluable servant to the city and freely gave of his knowledge for many schemes, particularly those involving water and roads. He was keenly interested in improving housing for the poorer people of Edinburgh.

In 1872 Falshaw was defeated by James Cowan in the election for Lord Provost, but two years later, when Cowan was elected to the House of Commons, Falshaw became Edinburgh's first citizen. A number of schemes were promoted during his term of office, including the Moorfoot Water Development, the Arboretum, opening West Princes Street Gardens to the public, roofing the Waverley Market, and widening both Princes Street and the North Bridge. The Falshaw Bridge over the Water of Leith at the west end of Glenogle Road is named after him.

Sir James declined to stand for Parliament but continued with his interest in railway development, being chairman of the North British Railway. He died in 1889 at the age of 79.

There is no doubt that the Queen's visit had created widespread interest, and the railway companies reported that it had been their busiest period since the 1861 Review. The North British Railway Company said that in addition to their scheduled timetable, when it had been necessary to include additional coaches, they had run 30 excursions, and the company estimated that 50,000 passengers had been carried into the city. These 'specials' came from Carlisle, Langholm, Berwickshire, Roxburghshire, East Lothian, Fife and the north. Trains also ran from Portobello, Dalkeith, Musselburgh and Roslin.

Eleven 'specials' arrived at West Princes Street station between 8 a.m. and 1 p.m. in addition to nine scheduled trains. The number of passengers was estimated at 15,000. Despite the vast volume of traffic all trains were running within a few minutes of advertised times.

Sir John Steell

Although born in Aberdeen in 1804, John Steell spent most of his life in Edinburgh. A childhood friend recalled an incident when the future sculptor was about eight years old and the two families lived 'on the steep road ascending to Calton Hill', where they played on the plainstanes (pavements). One day Steell suddenly

Alexander and Bucephalus in the quadrangle, City Chambers.

took a piece of chalk and in two or three strokes 'dashed off without the least apparent trouble, a figure of a galloping horse, of large size, so entirely different and to exceed in point of character and excellence anything that children ever did'.

Steell studied at Edinburgh and then went to Rome. On his return he quickly attracted attention by his magnificent Alexander and Bucephalus which was sited on the west side of St Andrew Square. In 1917 it was removed to its present location in the quadrangle at the City Chambers, to make way for the Gladstone Memorial. Gladstone was in turn repositioned in Coates Crescent during the mid-1950s, as he was causing traffic congestion in St Andrew Square.

Attempts were made to entice Steell to London for the reason that no commission for an important public statue in bronze or

The Wellington statue, east end of Princes Street.

marble had been given to a sculptor in Scotland. He elected to remain in Scotland with considerable success and was appointed Queen Victoria's sculptor in Scotland in 1838. He is also credited with having introduced artistic bronze casting into Scotland.

Many examples of Steell's work can be seen in the vicinity of Princes Street, including Wellington (at Register House); Sir Walter Scott and Professor John Wilson (in East Princes Street gardens); Queen Victoria (on the roof of the RSA building); Allan Ramsay (at the Mound entrance to West Princes Street gardens); Thomas Chalmers (junction of George Street/Castle Street); Prince Albert (Charlotte Square) and Viscount Melville (Melville Street/Crescent).

In addition, Steell completed statues of the Marquis of Dalhousie and the Rt Hon James Wilson, who started life as an apprentice hat manufacturer in Hawick, became a politician and

Allan Ramsay; at the Mound entrance to West Princes Street Gardens.

established the *Economist* newspaper, was financial member of the Council of India and introduced paper money into India. Both of these statues were for Calcutta. Steell was also commissioned to complete a copy of the sitting Scott and a Burns both for New York. He died in 1891.

The National Trust for Scotland and the Square

Charlotte Square was initially residential, but by the beginning of the present century there was a significant change to office use. The 4th Marquess of Bute was very conscious of the importance of retaining Adam's influence and in the early 1900s he was responsible for the restoration of 5, 6 and 7 Charlotte Square, which included returning the roof line to the architect's original elevation. Proprietors on the north side followed suit. In 1949, at

Thomas Chalmers. At the junction of George Street and Castle Street.

the invitation of the 5th Marquess of Bute, the National Trust for Scotland established offices at 5 Charlotte Square.

During the late 1980s there was evidence of a move away from the Square, no doubt influenced by the attraction of the modern open-plan offices with adequate facilities for new technology which were not available in older buildings and could only be achieved at the expense of severely damaging the fabric of these Georgian houses.

Following the death of the 5th Marquess of Bute in 1956, numbers 5, 6 and 7 Charlotte Square passed, through The National Land Fund procedures, into the ownership of the National Trust for Scotland in 1966, in part satisfaction of death duties. The 6th Marquess, a former President of the Trust, expressed the hope that Charlotte Square would become the Trust's permanent home. No.

The Secretary of State's Residence in Charlotte Square.

5 is the Trust's headquarters, No. 6 is leased as Secretary of State for Scotland's official residence and No. 7, the Georgian House, is open to the public, and visitors can view a fine interpretation of an original Charlotte Square house. Also at No. 7, the Trust have made available a flat as the official residence for the Moderator of the General Assembly of the Church of Scotland.

As proof of their commitment to safeguard the Square, the Trust announced in April 1996 that they had purchased six adjoining properties, numbers 26–31 Charlotte Square, with the express intention of carrying out major restoration. It is their intention to occupy these premises which are on the south side, as their headquarters. Exhibition and gallery facilities will be provided to encourage public access to the buildings. It has been acknowledged by the Trust that this initiative to restore Charlotte Square has been made possible only by the generous financial assistance of £3.7 million from the Heritage Lottery Fund and £700,000 from Historic Scotland towards acquisition costs. Four Trust headquarters premises which are located away from the Square will be sold in their £1.5 million contribution.

At the time of the announcement Mr Hamish Leslie Melville, Chairman of the National Trust for Scotland, said: 'This transaction

The south side of Charlotte Square, which will be restored.

is a major development for the National Trust for Scotland, for Edinburgh and for Charlotte Square'. He recalled that the financial assistance from the Heritage Lottery Fund was the second award made by them to the National Trust for Scotland within a year. In April 1995, the award of £10.2 million towards the purchase and endowment of the Mar Lodge Estate helped save the heart of the Cairngorms for the benefit of the nation.

Anthea Case, Director of the National Heritage Memorial Fund, said: 'We are delighted that the Heritage Lottery Fund is helping to regenerate part of Edinburgh's architectural heritage. This project will enable a greater public understanding and appreciation of one of the finest squares in Europe, now also part of a World Heritage Site'.

The National Trust for Scotland have also expressed their hope that Charlotte Square Garden will be restored to its original lay-out, including more appropriate design of railings, pavement and road surfaces. Hopefully, one day, visitors to Charlotte Square will see it as envisaged by its designer Robert Adam.

– 6 –
HOGMANAY — AND A POLICEMAN IS MURDERED

There would have been a certain degree of apprehension in the police office. It was Hogmanay, 1811, and who was to know what lay ahead as New Year's Day approached? Their fears were not without foundation, and about 11 p.m. reports were received that gangs of youths, armed with bludgeons, were roaming the streets, assaulting and robbing any pedestrians they encountered.

The gangs, numbering between forty and fifty youths, were reported to be in areas as far apart as the Bridges and Lochrin, and many perfectly innocent citizens were to suffer at the hands of these ruffians. Many required hospital treatment. Most sinister of all, however, was the assault on police officer Dugald Campbell who was attacked as he patrolled in the High Street, adjacent to Stamp Office Close. Campbell's injuries were serious and he was rushed to the Infirmary.

So seriously did the Town Council consider these outbreaks of violence that the following advertisement was placed in the *Evening Courant*:

REWARD OF 100 GUINEAS

Whereas outrages of a most violent nature, and hitherto unexampled in Edinburgh, have been committed last night upon several gentlemen and police officers, when passing along the streets by knocking them down, maltreating and robbing them.

The Lord Provost and Magistrates, in order to lead to a discovery of the persons concerned in those proceedings, hereby offer a reward of one hundred guineas to be paid to informers, upon conviction of the offender or offenders.

Several people were seized during the night, and brought before the Magistrates and Judge of Police, who were in attendance, and some articles were found in their possession which were supposed belong to persons who have been robbed.

It is requested that such will call at the Council-chamber, to give the requisite information, and to identify their property.

From the whole circumstances that came out, upon investigation last night, there appears to have been a regular plan of robbery previously concerted by the perpetrators, who were almost all boys or young lads, armed with bludgeons for the purpose.

As this is a thing so new in the metropolis, as well as flagrant in itself, the Lord Provost and Magistrates are determined to follow up the inquiry in the most rigorous manner, and they earnestly call upon all ranks of citizens, especially those who have the charge of apprentices and youths, to give every aid in their power, so as their most atrocious combination may be effectually detected, and a severe public example made of all those concerned in it.

The notice was signed by Lord Provost William Creech and four bailies. Creech was no stranger to criminal offences and served on the jury at the trial of Deacon Brodie in 1788.

But the situation took a more serious turn when police officer Campbell died on 5 January. Immediately a second notice appeared in the newspaper under the heading 'MURDER!', and the council offered an additional 100 guineas for information leading to the arrest and conviction of the person or persons concerned. Another note warned businessmen to beware of purchasing watches etc, which might have been stolen, and requesting people who had lost property to furnish all details to the council offices.

The drama continued to worsen with the death of a second man four days later. Under the heading 'ANOTHER MURDER', the paper informed its readers that James Campbell, a Leith clerk, had died from injuries received in the Hogmanay riots and that the reward had been increased by a further 100 guineas for information leading to a conviction.

In the same issue of the *Courant* a news item reported that some progress had been made in the police investigations with the arrest, in Glasgow, of Hugh McIntosh and Neil Sutherland. Following this encouraging progress, however, all leads went cold, and in an attempt to stimulate interest, the council, on 16 January, offered 50 guineas in return for information regarding the whereabouts of Hugh McDonald, aged 20, a shoemaker; James Johnstone, aged 17 or 18, a stonemason, and George Napier, a tanner. Meanwhile there was considerable criticism regarding the lack of progress being made by the police. No doubt the police were in possession of more information than was released to the public, arrests were made, and in due course there were court appearances.

The first trial took place on 2 March 1812, when John Skelton appeared before the High Court on three charges of robbery with violence. The first charge was deserted by the Crown, but the accused was found guilty on the other two counts and was sentenced to death.

Then, on 20 March, Hugh McIntosh, Neil Sutherland and Hugh McDonald appeared on 11 charges, the most serious of which was the murder of policeman Dugald Campbell. A fourth man, James Johnstone, had also been charged, but he had escaped from custody. Johnstone was declared an outlaw with a reward on his head.

As was usual at that time, the trial continued through to its finish and in this case, that was at 4 a.m. the following morning. The youths, whose ages ranged from 16 to 19, were found guilty and sentenced to be hanged in the High Street, immediately opposite Stamp Office Close where the unfortunate policeman had been murdered. It was further directed by the court that McIntosh's body should be delivered to the Professor of Anatomy to be dissected and anatomised.

The police, no doubt driven on by the severe criticism, pursued every minute lead and had a certain degree of success. On 31 March, George Napier and John Grotto appeared in court charged with being implicated in the murder of the policeman. They denied this serious charge which, had they been convicted, would certainly have resulted in being sentenced to death, but the pair admitted being involved in the robberies. Both were sentenced to 14 years transportation. At the same court Robert Gunn and Alexander McDonald pleaded guilty to six charges of robbery and were transported for life.

On 22 April, nearly four months after the crime had been committed, the tragic story of the Hogmanay murders drew to a close when scaffolding was erected at the head of Stamp Office Close. It was common in those days for the judge to order that executions be carried out at the scene of the crime — perhaps as a final reminder?

No trial had caught the attention of the Edinburgh public for a considerable number of years...and this was reflected in the massive crowds who were in the vicinity of the High Street as the appointed time for execution approached. The officials took every precaution to ensure that there would be no incidents.

The short distance from the Tolbooth to the scaffold was lined by 400 men from the Perth and Renfrewshire Militia. At 2.40 p.m. the procession, headed by the High Constables and followed by the magistrates in their robes and carrying the rods of office, left the Tolbooth and walked slowly to the place of execution. They were followed by the three condemned men , although 'men' is perhaps a wrong description, for Hugh McDonald, Hugh McIntosh and Neil Sutherland were never to see their eighteenth birthday. They were comforted by ministers of religion as they walked through that frightening mob, and Hugh McDonald carried a Bible. Devotion at the scaffold lasted for 45 minutes and finally, at a signal from Sutherland, society gained its revenge. Sutherland and McDonald had agreed that the sentence was just, but McIntosh went to his death protesting his innocence and denied any part in the murders.

The sight of a triple hanging, alas, appealed to the ghoulish nature of a vast number of Edinburgh's citizens and it was reported that never had such a crowd assembled in the High Street. It is also claimed that the proceedings were stage-managed in such a manner as to warn the youth of the Scottish capital of the consequences should they dare repeat the offences which took place on that Hogmanay/New Year's Day period which ushered out 1811 and welcomed 1812 in such a riotous way.

The authorities had taken a calculated chance in organising such a high-profile execution, for there was a very great risk of trouble. But the plans had been laid carefully. In addition to the troops who lined the route, 200 members of the 1st Royal Edinburgh Volunteers and a company of sharpshooters were stationed discreetly in Parliament Square; the 1st Edinburgh Militia were located in Hunter's Square while the 6th Dragoons were within easy call of the area. They were not needed. Edinburgh's citizens caused no trouble. Perhaps the city's high profile approach to the occasion had been the correct one.

– 7 –
MOB RULE IN THE WEST BOW

Historic Greyfriars churchyard contains a fine collection of centuries-old, ornate gravestones which serve as reminders of some of Edinburgh's famous, wealthy, and distinguished citizens. Almost certainly, however, the stone most likely to be missed by the casual visitor is a long, plain and simple memorial, now partly covered in a green deposit making the inscription difficult to decipher. Close inspection will reveal the name John Porteous and, more sinisterly, a word rarely seen on a gravestone — 'Murdered'. The full wording on the memorial reads: 'John Porteous a Captain of the Edinburgh City Guard Murdered 7 September, 1736. All Passion Spent 1973'. For more than 200 years, this has been the Porteous resting place, and for most of that time the grave has been marked by nothing more than a wooden post. This is not surprising, for his death, despised as the man was, is remembered as one of the most shameful incidents in Edinburgh's history and resulted in the Government taking reprisals against the Scottish capital.

The incidents leading up to what became known as the Porteous Riots were relatively straightforward and the year 1736 had opened relatively quietly in Edinburgh with no hint of the drama that was to follow. Petty smuggling was an 'occupation' followed by more than a few men, and from time to time the law-breakers were apprehended by the Customs officers. Such was the fate of Andrew Wilson from Pathhead, near Kirkcaldy, who, aggrieved by the seizure of his contraband, resolved to recover at least the equivalent value of the appropriated property.

Consequently, on 9 January 1736, Wilson, accompanied by George Robertson of Bristo Port, Edinburgh, and a number of associates, robbed the Collector at Pittenweem of a sum of money. Curiously the robbery had been carried out so openly that Wilson and Robertson were arrested the same evening and the money recovered. In due course the pair stood trial in Edinburgh and were condemned to death — a sentence which the citizens of Edinburgh considered to be severe.

The pair were incarcerated in the Tolbooth, and in accordance with the custom of that period, on the Sunday prior to the date set for their execution, the condemned men were taken to St Giles' Cathedral for the church service, accompanied by four guards. Suddenly Wilson seized two of the soldiers, at the same time yelling at Robertson to make his escape. Robertson vaulted the pews, and almost as if by a prepared plan the congregation stood aside and allowed the prisoner to go clear. At this Wilson calmly sat down. There was no doubt where the sympathy of the Edinburgh citizens lay, and there was considerable anxiety among the town officials as 14 April — the date fixed for the execution — approached. Concerned that an attempt might be mounted to rescue the second man, the magistrates ordered that the guard be doubled and that the officers and men of the Trained Bands be in attendance at the execution. In addition, the City Guard were each issued with three shots and by special order the weapons were loaded before marching off on duty.

As 2 p.m. (the time set for the death penalty to be carried out) approached, a battalion of regular troops then billeted in the Canongate, were drawn up on each side of the Lawnmarket. In addition, reserve soldiers under arms were on call in the guard-room. A vast crowd had assembled in the Grassmarket to witness the execution. The sentence was carried out, and confusing stories have been told regarding what followed. It was alleged that as the hangman mounted a ladder to release the body he was stoned by a number of boys. This was not an unusual occurrence on such occasions, but it is said that several of the guard were struck and nerves were already on a knife-edge.

The guard was under the command of Captain John Porteous, the son of a respectable Canongate tailor who had followed his father's profession for a time before choosing to join the army as a career. In 1718, having left the army, he was appointed adjutant of the City Guard and eight years later he reached the rank of captain. This promotion was surprising, for Porteous was an un-popular man with a violent temper and sadistic character. In July, 1735, he allegedly quarrelled with a fellow officer, John Fergusson, and the pair came to blows while appearing before the Town Council. They were dismissed from their posts but later reinstated.

It was rumoured that Porteous was extremely angry at Robertson's escape and that he had been particularly brutal to

Wilson on the days before the execution. The stone-throwing was the opportunity that Porteous had been seeking and he grabbed a weapon from one of the men and began firing wildly.

By the time the shooting was over four spectators were dead (and two injured persons subsequently died) and eleven more were injured but survived. Some of the victims were not even in the crowd but were looking on from nearby windows, which illustrates how indiscriminate the firing had been. Porteous retreated his men up the West Bow and to the guard-room. At the outset he could have read the Riot Act but he had chosen not to do so. His duties completed, the captain made his way to the Spread Eagle Tavern where the magistrates were already assembled.

Captain John Porteous was not above the law and he was charged with murder. Porteous emphatically denied the charge claiming that he had not given an order to shoot into the crowd, nor had he fired his weapon. The three shots, authorised by the magistrates were still in his possession — two in his cartridge-box and the other in his firearm. The commanding officer was taken to the Council Chamber, questioned at length and charged with murder.

Porteous was brought to trial on 19 July 1736 and despite his protestations he was sentenced to death with the execution date fixed for 8 September. The trial had been a lengthy one, and had continued non-stop. It did not conclude until 9 a.m. the following morning, and Porteous had to wait a further seven hours before he was to learn his fate.

An appeal was immediately dispatched to London where, in the absence of George II, Queen Caroline ordered a stay of execution. This news reached Edinburgh on 2 September.

Once more the wrath of Edinburgh was roused, and within a short space of time it was being whispered in the coffee-houses that Porteous would die on the date decreed by the court. On 7 September a message was delivered to Lord Provost Alexander Wilson, warning him of the serious situation; but no action was taken. At approximately 9 p.m. that night the rioters assembled at Portsburgh, and, preceded by a drummer, marched through the Grassmarket, increasing in number at every step. They quickly overpowered the City Guard and then turned their attention to the Tolbooth, where, with some difficulty, they gained entry.

With the crowd in this mood it was impossible to find anyone who was prepared to carry a message, but finally the Lord Provost persuaded Patrick Lindsay, the town's Member of Parliament, to make contact with General Moyes, who was in command of the garrison. This military gentleman refused to act on the basis of a verbal message.

It was now 11.30 and the mob had gained access to the prison, where they took the keys from a terrified warder. The luckless Porteous was soon identified by the lynch mob and dragged by way of the West Bow to the Grassmarket. They stopped briefly at the foot of the Bow where a shop was entered and a rope procured for the hanging; very considerately a guinea was left to pay for the noose. In the darkness, the rioters, carrying torches, manhandled their prisoner to the south side of the Grassmarket, directly opposite the West Bow. There they found a dyer's pole over which they threw the rope. In a flash it was round the condemned man's neck and mob justice was carried out. Quickly and quietly the rioters dispersed, leaving on the ground the weapons they had stolen from the armoury.

The 'sentence' on John Porteous had been carried out in a most barbaric manner and death followed after several abortive attempts. The victim fought ferociously to the end. It was not until several hours later that the authorities were prepared to venture into the Grassmarket and recover the body of the former Captain of the City Guard. He was later laid to rest in Greyfriars.

Not surprisingly there was panic among the town's officials for they knew that on this occasion they were answerable to London. When the full facts of what had taken place reached the southern capital they were received with anger, tempered by a degree of horror. The King, who was in Hanover, was kept informed by way of a series of express messages. A hurried meeting of the magistrates was convened at which it was decided to put on a show of power. As a message to London the council ordered the arrest of anyone remotely suspect. More than 200 people were taken into custody, questioned, and then released because of lack of evidence. But a question much discussed among the law-abiding citizens concerned the unusually large number of strangers who had appeared in the town hours before the riots began. The council were well aware that a disturbance was a strong possibility, and why weren't the City Guard instructed to monitor their movements? Perhaps they had been, but then their commanding officer was not exactly the most popular of superiors. And where were these visitors now? Had they left the town as quietly and quickly as they had appeared? Perhaps they were nothing more that morbid spectators.

London too was most anxious to bring the perpetrators to justice, and a number of officials (including General Wade) were sent to Edinburgh to assist the Lord Advocate with his enquiries.

A proclamation was issued offering a reward of £200 (a vast amount of money) for information leading to the conviction of anyone involved, but no-one was tempted. The message was to be read on the first Sunday of each month in the churches for a year; but all was in vain. A Bill was introduced in the House of Lords 'to disable Alexander Wilson, Esq., Lord Provost of the City of Edinburgh, from taking, holding or enjoying any office or place of magistracy in the City of Edinburgh or anywhere in Great Britain and also for imprisoning him; for abolishing the town guard and removing the gates at the Netherbow Port'.

The Lord Provost was arrested on 1 April and spent three weeks in prison before being granted bail. In due course he, and four bailies with the Lords of Justiciary, were ordered to appear before the House of Lords. Immediately there was a problem — protocol. On their arrival at the Lords there was a debate on whether the Scottish Justiciary Lords should attend in their robes and whether at the table or the bar! It was claimed that as this point had not been settled by the articles of Union it was their right to be seated beside the English judges. After a lengthy discussion it was determined that the Scottish legal representatives should appear in their robes at the bar; but they insisted that it was their right to appear within the bar.

The Bill to punish Edinburgh for its misdemeanours was fought vigorously by the Scottish Members of Parliament, and following numerous amendments, passed through both the Lords and Commons.

The clauses to imprison the Lord Provost, abolish the City Guard and remove the Netherbow gates were omitted and replaced with a fine of £2,000, this sum to benefit the widow of the luckless Captain John Porteous. But the action also cost the town's tax payers £1446:2:7½ exclusive of lawyers' fees. Considering what the consequences might have been, the

No. 89 West Bow. Legend has it that from this shop was obtained the rope to hang Captain Porteous.

Edinburgh officials returned well-satisfied with the outcome. Citizens turned out in great numbers and travelled miles to the east of the town to meet the party. Lord Provost Alexander Wilson, by nature a quiet man, got word of what was going on and returned to Edinburgh by a different route. Wilson ceased to be Lord Provost on 13 July 1737, by virtue of Act of Parliament, and he was succeeded by Archibald Macauley six days later.

Little remains of the old West Bow, although number 89, traditionally the shop where the rioters obtained the rope from Mrs Jeffrey's premises, has survived. It is still a retail shop. But until as recently as thirty years ago you could still buy all types of ropes and twines from 89 West Bow, then occupied by William

Bell (Ropes) Ltd. Not long before the shop closed I called to see the manager, Alexander Livingston. As I looked around the premises there lay bundles of ropes and twines which to the casual visitor may have looked untidy, but Mr Livingston knew exactly where anything could be located.

The shop counter, a substantial piece of dark, solid wood, stood just inside the door. It looked very old and marked from years of service and as my eyes moved along the flat, scored surface my thoughts automatically turned to the story of the Porteous Riots. Suddenly, and to my amazement, there, embedded on the counter was an old coin...surely not... Mr Livingston anticipated what I was thinking and explained the mystery:

> When I came to the shop in the early 1950s an old battered farthing was screwed to the counter. It was rather unsightly, and when a friend gave me five old-looking but worthless coins, I decided to remove the farthing and replace it with one of the newly-acquired coins. Over the years four of these coins were stolen but if the characters who removed them thought that they were inheriting the golden guinea the laugh was on theme for, in fact, they were worthless counterfeit coins used by gamblers in years gone by!

At the time of my last visit the fifth and last coin lay fixed in place with little chance of it being removed.

'You see' said Mr Livingston with a laugh, 'every day for a week after I had put it in place, I applied layers of jewellers' glue just to make quite sure!'.

Number 89 West Bow was a popular tourist attraction and for nearly 20 years the shop manager had a constant flow of visitors, not so much concerned about purchasing a length of rope (for legitimate purposes of course), but with the business transaction completed, the story of the shop and its traditional connection with the death of Porteous. Visitors would call in from all over the world, particularly from America and Australia. But there was always a fair number of children with an interest in local history.

When, on the last working day of 1967, Alexander Livingston closed the door at 89 West Bow, it brought to an end an important link in Edinburgh's history and tradition. After more than 230 continuous years, a shop which had sold ropes and twines to countless generations of Edinburgh citizens would no longer provide this service.

No doubt Mr Livingston's final act was to take a last nostalgic look round the now empty premises. But were they empty? Within these four walls there surely remained centuries of memories — not least the mystery surrounding the identity of the rioters who, on 7 September 1736, smashed open the door, took a length of rope, and, leaving payment on the counter, then dragged the terrified Captain John Porteous to face his death on a dyer's pole, just across the road in the Grassmarket.

– 8 –
THE NIGHT THE
ZEPPELIN BOMBERS STRUCK

When the Lord Provost's Sub-Committee 'A' met at the City Chambers on 18 February 1916, they were acutely aware that air attacks on Edinburgh and Leith were strong possibilities; Zeppelins had already bombed areas of England causing death and damage.

The meeting chaired by Lord Provost Robert K. Inches, had been convened to consider two items: (1) The Lights (Scotland) No. 1 Order which had been issued by the Secretary of State for Scotland on 9 February 1916, under the Provisions of the Defence of the Realm Regulations, and (2) a motion by Councillor Lorne Macleod in the following terms: 'To consider anew the arrangements for the City in connection with Aircraft Invasion'.

The committee were advised and noted that in the event of intimation being received by the police that hostile aircraft were within a certain distance of the city, the electric light in the streets would be turned down to a dull glow, not visible from the aircraft, and likewise it would be turned down in private houses where electricity was used. This, if the intimation was received after dark, would be a warning to people in the street and to those in the houses where there was electric light, that an attack was imminent. As no gas lamps in the streets were lit, nothing needs to be done with them. It was not practicable to turn off quickly the supply of gas to those houses which use gas, so they would not get a corresponding warning to that given to electric light users. It was pointed out that if an attack was launched late at night the lights might not be on and the residents in bed. Consequently, the first evidence of the presence of enemy raiders would be when bombs were dropped.

The committee went on to consider the question of providing audio warning, possibly by the use of hooters, buzzers or sirens, but the councillors decided that any of these methods were unnecessary and undesirable. There had been a Zeppelin raid at Southend and as the siren sounded crowds rushed into the streets to watch the attacker. Evidence given at coroners' inquests in England proved that most casualties were in the street. It had also been proved that the use of a sound warning could be beneficial to the enemy. At Southend a Zeppelin passed over the darkened city, unaware of the town below. The raider returned when the crew picked up the sound of the siren which had been installed at the electric light works to warn the inhabitants. Bombs were then dropped on the town.

There had also been instances of warnings being sounded, causing alarm among the citizens, but with no attack taking place. And in big communities, it was pointed out, 'there are always many persons who have weak hearts or are in dangerous stages of illness to whom great excitement might prove injurious or fatal'.

It was interesting that the Secretary of State had not taken the responsibility of recommending or ordering these to be used but had left local authorities to make their own decisions. The Chief Constable, Roderick Ross, was strongly against the use of audible warning.

After lengthy discussion, the sub-committee approved unanimously: (1) that it was not expedient to give the public warning of a possible air attack by sound signals; (2) that the Chief Constable be authorised to advise the public accordingly, and, (3) the contents of the notices which he proposed to insert in the newspapers and circulate by means of handbills to be delivered to every house and by way of posters exhibited at certain places.

The citizens of Edinburgh and Leith did not have long to wait, and the authorities' worst fears were realised when at approximately 11.25 p.m. on Sunday 2 April 1916, a Zeppelin was sighted crossing the Firth of Forth west of Inchkeith and travelling in a south-westerly direction towards Leith Docks. Shortly afterwards a bomb was dropped at the west end of the Edinburgh Dock, sinking two rowing boats and breaking skylights in two Danish sailing vessels. The Albert Dock was the next target where incendiary bombs fell on the quay and a nearby yard. Both fires were quickly extinguished. Soon afterwards an explosive hit Watt & Jackson's grain warehouse at Timber Bush. Damage was done to the roof and part of the wall at a high level, resulting in masonry falling on to the adjoining properties, causing considerable damage. A wall at the edge of the harbour Quay and close to the

Custom House was struck and the blast blew in a considerable number of windows in dwellinghouses, shops and offices in the vicinity.

The enemy then turned their attention to the civilian population and a bomb fell at 2 Commercial Street, destroying part of the tenement roof and wall. Robert Love, aged 66, was killed by shrapnel as he lay in bed. An incendiary pierced the roof of the tenement at 14 Commercial Street, into a room occupied by an elderly woman and through the floor into the flat below, where it exploded in flames. According to the contemporary police report, the woman calmly got out of bed, poured water through the hole made by the bomb 'and thus prevented a serious fire'. Minor damage was also done at 45 Sandport Street, and a bomb which landed on the pavement at 9 Sandport Street did no damage.

Not so lucky was the Innes & Grieve whisky bond where an explosive hit the building, which was completely destroyed. The estimated loss (including contents) was £44,000 and there was no cover for this type of damage. Nearby premises were damaged by the blast.

And still the rampage continued. An incendiary struck the dwellings at 15 Church Street, damaging a house occupied by a soldier, his wife and three children. It then penetrated the floor into the downstairs flat where a man and wife and five children were at home. Although both premises were set alight and considerable damage done, fortunately no one was injured.

Not so lucky was the minister who lived at St Thomas Church manse in Mill Lane where the thirteenth bomb to be dropped in Leith almost completely destroyed the house causing an estimated £1,000 damage. The Minister, his wife and servant had retired for the night and had a 'miraculous' escape! Unfortunately the manse was not insured against enemy action.

Leith Hospital in Mill Lane had a close call with a bomb falling on the gravel to the front of the building, but there was no damage; nor was there any problem with a similar incident in the playgound of the adjacent St Thomas School. A short time later explosive bombs were dropped at 200 Bonnington Road. One fell in the court breaking windows and damaging doors. Alas, the one-year-old son of Robert Robb was killed as he lay in bed. He was struck by a piece of shell, which, it is believed, entered the bedroom by way of a window. An explosive landed on the railway line near

Bonnington tannery and failed to explode, but a second damaged the leather manufacturing tank.

On 7 April 1916, the Leith Chief Constable, in response to a Scottish Office letter dated 5 April, said:

> The only warning given to the population of this town of an approach by enemy aircraft was the lowering of the electric light and as the electric light is not general only a small percentage of the inhabitants received the warning. The public feeling is that the users of gas should be put on the same footing with the users of electricity. If it were practicable to manipulate the gas supply in the same manner as electricity it would ease the public mind as it is quite evident that the people consider it more secure in the open than in their dwellings. Personally I think the less people know about the presence of enemy aircraft, the better.

The Chief Constable also drew attention to the large number of ships lying in Leith Roads, fully lighted and visible from a long distance. He wrote:

> A better guide for a Zeppelin could not be got. On the night of the raid the Zeppelin came to Leith across the line of the shipping and not till the bombs were falling on Leith were the lights on the ships extinguished. It seems so ridiculous to have the town of Leith in darkness while the sea in front of it is illuminated. This illumination in the Firth of Forth is causing great uneasiness among the inhabitants of this town. Something should be done before this state of uneasiness breaks out into indignation.

The Scottish Office response was swift, and on 10 April they wrote to the Chief Constable stating that the Secretary of State had contacted the Admiralty regarding the lighting of shipping off Leith. Orders had been issued 'prohibiting the docking and undocking of merchant ships at Leith during the hours of official night...No lights of any description visible from outboard will be permitted in mercantile shipping anchored in the Leith and Granton roadsteads'.

In a report dated 12 April 1916, by the Leith Chief Constable to the Scottish Office at Whitehall, he said:

> From the position in which the bombs were dropped it is evident that those in charge of the Zeppelin were following the course of the Water of Leith from Leith Docks to Edinburgh as the bombs dropped

were not more than 100 yards from the said Water of Leith at any point except the one dropped in the Edinburgh Dock.

There were a great number of premises rendered insecure through the breaking of glass in windows, doors etc., by the explosion of the bombs and although goods in many cases were exposed, not one case of pilfering has been reported to the police. Though the inhabitants rushed into the streets their conduct was on the whole very good. The authorised police force was assisted by 250 special constables who gave valuable assistance.

The Chief Constable of Midlothian reported that a bomb had been dropped at Longstone, Slateford, Parish of Colinton, when the windows of 23 dwellinghouses were broken. The cost of the damage was estimated at £5. A bomb was dropped the same night at Cameron Bank Dairy, Peffermill Road, in the Parish of Liberton. The windows of two houses were broken and the cost of replacing them was £1.

At 7 p.m. on 2 April, the telephone rang in the Edinburgh City Police HQ. It was a message from the Post Office instructing them 'to be prepared to take action'. The wording would have been meaningless to the general public, but it was immediately recognised by the police as a pre-arranged signal from the military authorities warning of a possible air raid.

Two hours and five minutes later came the second part of the message: 'Take air raid action'. Immediately the police put their plan into operation. The electric light department were instructed to lower all lights which would warn the public of an impending air attack.

All traffic was stopped, and the lights on vehicles were extinguished. The Central Fire Station and Red Cross were alerted. Police stations were informed, and all men then off duty were ordered to report. The Special Force were also called out.

At 11.50 p.m. bombs were reported to be exploding in the Leith area, and from that time until about 12.25 a.m. on Monday 3 April, 24 bombs — 18 high explosive and 6 incendiaries — fell on Edinburgh.

The first indication that the city was under direct attack was when a high explosive bomb fell on vacant land at Bellevue Terrace. Although there were no reported injuries, front and rear windows were blown-out in twenty houses in the terrace. In addition window damage affected the tenement at 48 and 50

Rodney Street and nine shops in the street; Heriot Hill Terrace, Cornwallis Place, Summer Place, Canonmills School and Neil's Printing works. Bellevue Parish Church had seven windows broken.

An incendiary landed on the Mound, four hundred yards from the castle, but caused no damage.

There was a serious incident at Lauriston Place when a high explosive bomb hit the house at No. 39, occupied by Dr John McLaren, wrecking the roof and the wall which divided the house from No. 41. Although both premises were occupied, no one was injured. Unfortunately David Robertson (aged 27) a discharged soldier who lived a 4 Graham (now Keir) Street, was walking in the vicinity at the time of the bombing in this area, was struck in the stomach by a piece of shrapnel and subsequently died at the Infirmary.

George Watson's College, which at that time was located in Archibald Place, Lauriston, suffered damage internally and also to windows and stonework when a bomb was dropped in the playground. After inspection by the college authorities the decision was taken to close the building for a week for repairs to be carried out. The incident had its lighter moments, none more so than when the pupils discovered that they were to have an unexpected holiday. Subsequently a plaque was placed on the outside wall, close to where the bomb had fallen. It read: 'This city was raided by a German airship on the night of April 2 1916. Near this spot a bomb exploded causing serious damage to the college buildings'. When the former school was demolished the plaque was salvaged and taken to the new building in Colinton Road where it is displayed on a classroom wall as a reminder of that dramatic night in April 1916.

Many windows were destroyed at the Royal Infirmary and at nearby Chalmers Street. Then, at approximately 11.55 p.m. the raider crossed the Meadows where a bomb was dropped but caused no damage. Not so fortunate, however, was part of a tenement building in Marchmont Crescent where a high-explosive landed and exploded on impact. A large section of bomb careered through three flats and came to rest on the floor of the ground-floor flat next door.

An old tenement at 183 Causewayside, which consisted of single- and double-room houses on five flats was practically

External damage, George Watson's College, Archibald Place, Edinburgh
(Reproduced by kind permission of the Blair-Morrison Library, George
Watson's College).

wrecked. Access to the houses was by way of two stairs which
had been displaced and were in danger of collapsing. The front
outer wall had suffered greatest damage.

Remarkably, only six people were injured, including three of
the Porteous family. Rose Porteous and Private Thomas Porteous
(aged 17), who was home, on leave, were detained in the
Infirmary. Also detained was Jessie Halkett. Two-months-old
Beatrice Pinkerton was described as suffering from 'slight shock'.

Incendiaries were dropped in the rear gardens at Hatton Place
and Blacket Place but no damage was inflicted.

The White Hart Hotel, 34 Grassmarket, suffered considerable
damage caused by a bomb which landed on the pavement.
Windows were blown out on both sides of the Grassmarket, West
Bow and West Port. Four people were injured, including William

A wrecked classroom, George Watson's College, Archibald Place, Edinburgh (Reproduced by kind permission of the Blair-Morrison Library, George Watson's College).

Breakey, 45-year-old carter who lived at the Corn Exchange Buildings. He was struck by a section of bomb and died later in the Infirmary.

There was also an attempt to destroy the castle — perhaps it was being used as a military hospital? The high explosive fell on the south-west rock but the castle survived, although windows in Castle Terrace, Spittal Street and Grindlay Street were destroyed. At the spot where the bomb exploded there is a plaque which, over the years has blended with the rock and foliage. I located it by using binoculars and it reads: 'On this spot a bomb fell during the German air raid — 2nd April, 1916'.

While it is important that this plaque should remain *in situ*, would it not be wise for the appropriate authority to erect a second plate, beside the pathway?

This plaque, erected at George Watson's College, Archibald Place, as a reminder of the First war air attack was later removed to the new Watson's College in Colinton Road.

Perhaps it could read: 'A bomb fell near this spot during the Zeppelin raid on the night of 2/3 April, 1916'. Apart from identifying the location it might also prevent inquisitive people from scaling the steep embankment as they try to find the site.

Round the corner at 21 Lothian Road, the County Hotel took the full force of the attack. Although only one person was injured, the hotel roof was destroyed, while the rear wall and eighteen rooms were damaged. The hotel at 31 Lothian Road was also affected by the bombing.

In the valley of the Water of Leith, near Coltbridge Gardens, a dovecot was demolished and the embankment washed away. Windows were damaged at Coltbridge Gardens, Belford Place and Park, Douglas Crescent and Magdala Crescent. Twenty-eight windows were blasted out at Donaldson's Hospital and the author, Robert T. Skinner, was to write many years later: 'The oriel window at the north end of the chapel used to contain the earliest specimen in Scotland of figure-stained glass, that window with the other chapel windows being destroyed during the Zeppelin raid of 3rd. April 1916'.

Marshall Street, however, was the area that took the brunt of the attack and suffered the greatest number of casualties. A bomb fell opposite No. 16, totally destroying the houses on first floor, staircase and cellar. Other properties in the vicinity suffered damage to a lesser degree. Casulties were high and severe with six immediately reported dead and seven injured. Those who perished were: William Smith (aged 15), waiter; John Smith (aged 45), tinsmith; Henry George Rumble (aged 17), occupation unknown; Victor McFarlane (age unknown) hotel waiter; and David Thomas Graham (aged 5) who all lived at 16 Marshall Street, and William Ewing (aged 23), 33 Marshall Street. Those who suffered injuries were aged between three and seventy years, and included Private Thomas Donoghue (aged 24), 3/4 The Royal Scots who was stationed at Loanhead. He died at the Royal Infirmary on 10 April.

But still the havoc continued. In nearby Haddow's Court, Nicolson Street, an explosive device damaged some of the property. Three people were injured, one severely, and six days after the attack, 74-year-old James Farquhar died. The premises of D.&J. McCallum, Spirit Merchants, were demolished, while windows in Haddow's Court, Nicolson Street and Simon Square suffered extensive damage.

It is only a short distance to the St Leonard's area and here, at 69 St Leonard's Hill, the staircase was wrecked and the building severely damaged. But worse, four-year-old Cora Edmond Bell was killed. Her mother Isabella (aged 36) and Alice, aged 2½ years, sister of the dead girl, were badly injured and detained in the Royal Infirmary.

Next the bombers turned their attention to the King's (Holyrood) Park, but, not surprisingly, the damage was minimal. A section of boundary wall was hit as was the roof of a bonded warehouse. The 'bond' also lost 341 panes of glass!

A comprehensive police report on the incidents of that night concluded that it had not been possible to obtain the exact time at which the various bombs had been dropped, and it was therefore difficult to say what exact course the attackers had taken. Mrs Lawson, who lived at Prestonfield Lodge, confirmed that she had seen two airships at 12.15 a.m., one a little higher than the other, in the King's (Holyrood) Park, at the time the bombs were dropped in the vicinity. The witness also said that a 'strong blinding' light had been displayed by one of the airships, which then turned towards the city centre. Pieces of the bombs which had been collected at various parts of the town were handed over to the military authorities for examination.

The police confirmed that 24 incidents had been logged. Eleven people died on that night of destruction, but the number who were injured is uncertain, this being a category which is difficult to define, in any case many who were injured did not seek medical attention.

In a letter to the Secretary of State for Scotland, dated 5 April, the Chief Constable wrote:

> It is really remarkable, having regard to the damage done, that the fatalities have been so small and had it not been that several persons in the case of the Marshall Street explosion came out of their houses and entered the common stair, the loss of life would have been reduced to three persons.

The night of 2/3 April 1916, had caused considerable concern in Edinburgh and on 6 April, the Lord Provost's Committee, as the War Emergency Committee, met at the City Chambers to consider matters arising in connection with the air raid.

The Town Clerk read a letter which, on the authority of the Lord Provost, had been sent to Viscount French, Commander-in-Chief Home Forces, seeking details regarding measures to be taken for the defence of the City. It was also revealed that the Lord Provost was in London and had arranged a meeting with French to discuss the matter.

There was also submitted to the Committee, correspondence to do with dangers arising from a factory in the City for the manufacture of explosives. The Lord Provost, while in London, had taken the opportunity to meet with officials from the Ministry of Munitions to express the Council's concern.

Chief Constable Ross reported on the police participation and the measures taken on the occasion of the air raid. He also said that, on the authority of the Magistrates, he had made arrangements for the funerals of certain of the victims, for the temporary accommodation of families who had been rendered homeless, and for the relief of victims of the raid who were in need of help.

A sub-committee of six was then appointed to consult with the Local Military Authorities in regard to the defence of the City and other matters.

This sub-committee reconvened the following day but, and no doubt for security reasons, the minute of that meeting simply reveals that the councillors had met with the military representatives.

The sub-committee also met with a deputation from the Gas Commission concerning the desirability of giving intimation of the approach of enemy air craft by shutting off or reducing the pressure of the gas supply. They decided to delay further consideration of the matter.

On 8 April the War Emergency Committee convened at the City Chambers and the first item on the agenda was a letter from the military authorities in response to the Lord Provost's written request for assurances regarding the defence of the Scottish Capital. That letter read.

> General Headquarters,
> Home Forces,
> Horse Guards,
> London, S.W.

6th. April, 1916

Sir,

I am directed by the Field Marshal Commanding-in-Chief, Home Forces, to acknowledge the receipt of your letter of the 3rd. instant, in which you refer to the fact that guns are not at present mounted for the defence of the City of Edinburgh, and in which you express your astonishment that this has not been done.

I am to say that the City of Edinburgh has not been forgotten, and that, when available, guns will be mounted for its defence; but I am also to point out that there are many other places which are of vital importance to the Country, and to the successful prosecution of the war, and that the City of Edinburgh is to be considered with these.

The Field Marshal also hopes you will understand that guns and lights cannot be provided at short notice, and that the fact that the aerial defence of the whole of the United Kingdom is not at present complete is not due to the want of recognition of its importance on the part of the Military Authorities, but to the unprepared state of the Country on the outbreak of War.

> I have the honour to be,
> Sir,
> Your obedient
> Servant,
> (Signed) F. Shaw
> Major General, General Staff, Home Forces

There were two other items on that agenda: (1) a deputation was introduced and heard from the Rotary Club as to the measures which might be taken for warning the public in the event of an air raid, and, (2) The Committee had under consideration the question of whether any further arrangement should be made for giving intimation of the approach to the City of enemy aircraft.

It was suggested that warning might be given to the users of gas, similar to that given to users of electricity.

After discussion, the Committee resolved to recommend to the Magistrates and Council that the Gas Commissioners be requested, on the appropriate signal being given by the police, to reduce the pressure if that could be done with safety.

The Committee further agreed that should the foregoing recommendation be approved, representation be made to the Leith Corporation suggesting that the same arrangement should be made in Leith.

It was not until 31 January 1917 that Leith revealed the cost of that night of disaster, and the figure was given as £56,156. This included the destruction of the Innes & Grieve Spirit Merchant's property for which the estimate was £44,000.

The Edinburgh figures were given in a letter dated 8 February 1917 from the Chief Constable to the Secretary of State for Scotland. The table was shown as follows:

1.	Lothian Road	£1100
2.	Castle Terrace	260
3.	Grassmarket	1190
4.	Lauriston Place	1600
5.	Archibald Place	2750
6.	Marshall Street	1325
7.	Haddow's Court	2830
8.	St. Leonard's Hill	920
9.	Causewayside	2550
10.	Coltbridge Terrace/ Donaldson's Hospital	1500
11.	King's Park	40
12.	Canonmills and Heriothill	380
		16,445
	Barricading, watching and lighting	195
		£16,640

Pitt Street, Leith. An unusual reminder of the 1914–18 War The wording above the sculpture reads 'The valour of the German culture 1914'.

As the zeppelins drifted and droned over Leith and Edinburgh and the horrors of war were brought home to the civilian population, few of those who wandered into the streets to speculate at the cigar-shaped objects could have been aware of the historical background which culminated in the production of these bombers. The name was derived from the German inventor, Count Ferdinand Von Zeppelin, who was born in 1838 and was a career soldier.

He retired from the army in the early 1890s and devoted his time to the study of air travel, producing his first aircraft in 1900. By 1910 there was a Zeppelin service operating between Berlin and Lake Constance. With the advent of the Great War, the zeppelins were adapted for military purposes and bombing raids were launched on several areas of Britain. Von Zeppelin died on 8 March 1917, eleven months after his aircraft made their attacks on Leith and Edinburgh. The use of airships was commercially abandoned in the 1930s.

– 9 –
MADELEINE SMITH AND
THE EDINBURGH CONNECTION

Slateford railway station is on the Waverley–Glasgow (Central) line and most passengers will give it little more than a cursory glance. But observant travellers making a similar journey early on the summer evening of 9 July 1857, might have spotted a small, slightly-built young woman standing discreetly on the platform watching anxiously for the Glasgow-bound train. She wore a long silk dress, cloak, straw bonnet with dark ribbons and a green veil; and she was accompanied by a young man — her brother.

That woman was Madeleine Smith, who, three-and-a-half hours previously, had been sensationally freed from Edinburgh's High Court after a jury had returned a not-proven verdict on a charge of murder by poisoning her lover, Pierre L'Angelier. The trial had lasted for nine days and was one of the most notable cases of the nineteenth century.

Madeleine and Pierre were a socially unacceptable couple in Victorian Britain. She, only 21-years of age, from a prosperous family background which included a boarding-school education; he a clerk and ten years her senior.

The son of a Jersey nurseryman, L'Angelier came to Edinburgh in 1842. He was employed by Dickson & Co., the well-known seedsmen, before moving to Glasgow. He met Madeleine, and there followed a strange and protracted liaison; occasional meetings at her home when the family and servants were asleep, and through a lengthy series of letters. The correspondence began in 1855, she posting her letters, he delivering the replies by way of her bedroom window to avoid her parents' attention.

Madeleine soon tired of the association and attempted to end it, but the meetings and letter-writing continued. Eventually the couple became secretly engaged.

The situation became more complicated when, in January, 1857, Madeleine, with the approval of her family, accepted a proposal of marriage from neighbour William Minnoch. She broke off the affair with L'Angelier and attempted to recover her letters.

Unsuccessful, she purchased poisons which, the prosecution were to claim, she gave to her suitor during their secret meetings.

The trial opened at the High Court, Edinburgh, on 30 June 1857, when Madeleine Smith faced charges of administering, or causing to be administered, arsenic or some other poison with intent to murder and in fact to murder. Professor Frederick Penny told the court that he had carried out a post-mortem on L'Angelier and traces of arsenic had been found in the body — more than would be required to cause death.

Ann Jenkins, the dead man's landlady, said that one mid-February morning she suspected that her tenant was seriously ill. He had been violently sick, was yellow and 'dull', and complained of a thirst. About 4 a.m. on 22 February he had called for assistance, again saying that he had severe stomach pain. The landlady confirmed that L'Angelier received a large number of letters in yellow or white envelopes. She also noticed, in his room, a photograph of a young lady. 'Is that your intended, sir?', she had asked. 'Perhaps one day', he replied.

Mrs Jenkins also revealed that in September 1856, L'Angelier had asked to rent a dining-room and bedroom, explaining that he would be marrying the following March.

On 19 March, L'Angelier left for Bridge of Allan. He had expected to be away for about a week and had asked that any letters be forwarded to him immediately. A letter was delivered and redirected, and by Sunday, 22 March, he was back in Glasgow. L'Angelier went out that night about 9 p.m. returned at approximately 2 a.m., and, despite being in possession of a key, he rang the door bell 'violently'. He was sick throughout the night and despite receiving medical attention he died some hours later. Subsequently Mrs Jenkins asked William Stevenson, the dead man's boss, to take care of his effects. The suit that L'Angelier had worn on that fateful night was lying across a sofa and a search of the pockets revealed a number of trivial items, but most importantly, a letter. It was the one which had been re-addressed to Bridge of Allan, had been written by Madeleine Smith and had resulted in L'Angelier returning to Glasgow — and his death.

Madeleine Smith made a lengthy statement before a sheriff in which she admitted that she had known the deceased for about two years; had not seen him for three weeks before his death;

that they wrote to each other; had agreed to marry and that she had passed cocoa to him through her bedroom window. She also identified certain letters and admitted to purchasing arsenic for use as a cosmetic but denied having administered arsenic or anything injurious.

The jury retired at 1.10 p.m. on the ninth day of the trial for what was expected to be a protracted absence. After all there was almost nine days' evidence to consider in what many believed was a complicated trial. The jury thought otherwise, however, and after being out for only 22 minutes, they returned to the court with their verdicts. They were delivered to a highly charged High Court. The verdict was 'not proven' on the charge of murder, nor was she convicted on the other two charges.

While the verdicts were being read the prisoner gazed at the jury showing no emotion and when the verdict of 'not proven' on the third charge (that of murder) was given her head moved slightly downwards and her solemn face briefly gave way to a smile: — no doubt of relief.

Prolonged cheering filled the courtroom and this was behaviour rarely experienced in such surroundings. Attempts by the judge and court officials to restore order were unsuccessful . That is, until the Lord Justice Clerk spotted a man who was particularly enthusiastic and, as was pointed out to a policeman, he had a newspaper in his hand; as one periodical explained 'a newspaper too of the lowest character as might be inferred from the sequel'.

After the accused had been dismissed and a more relaxed attitude returned to the court-room the Lord Justice Clerk asked:

'Is that young man in custody? Bring him to the bar'.

The miscreant was placed before the bar, immediately opposite the presiding judge. His Lordship, having adjusted his glasses and studied the offender for a few seconds, addressed him in this manner:

This court has ordered you to the bar as an offender against the rules; but after looking at you, we do not think you are worthy to stand even in that position. You appear a very stupid person. Foolish, silly fellow, go away!

But the excitement of the day was not yet over and while the 'silly fellow' was being dealt with there were scenes outside the High Court familiar to readers of present-day tabloids but certainly unusual in the early Victorian era. They were graphically reported in one contemporary newspaper:

> In order to get rid of the mob assembled in Parliament Square, a ruse was resorted to, previous to Miss Smith's departure. A girl, in consideration of having her curiosity satisfied with a look of the ex-prisoner, agreed to perform the part of Miss Smith leaving the Court and, being suitably dressed and veiled, was hurried into the cab which had been procured for the purpose; but so affected was she by the eager gaze of the mob that she immediately fainted, and in that condition was driven down towards the jail, accompanied by a vociferating multitude,

That Madeleine Smith was given exceptional privilege is evident. After she had been dismissed from the Court she was taken to one of the witness-rooms where she changed her outer clothing. She remained in that room until just after four o'clock when she was taken upstairs, and through the building before leaving by way of the Exchequer office door. Then, accompanied by her brother, Madeleine Smith walked casually to the High Street where transport was waiting outside St Giles' It was a relatively short drive to Slateford railway station, which was on the Caledonian line. After a brief, anxious delay, the Smiths boarded the 5 p.m. train to Glasgow. Eventually arriving at Greenock, the tired couple embarked on a steamer for the journey to their father's residence at Rhu (it was spelt 'Row' in those days) and hopefully out of the limelight.

Madeleine Smith lived a very long time with her memories of that trial. Seventy-one years in fact, for she reportedly died in New York in 1928, aged ninety-two.

– 10 –
PAUL JONES AND A
THREATENED ATTACK ON LEITH

On Sunday 17 September 1779, Leith was in danger of attack. As the residents of the town worked frantically to prepare defences, the 40-gun *Bon Homme Richard* under the command of Paul Jones together with the support vessels *Vengeance* and *Pallas* lay off Inchkeith.

But quite unexpectedly the danger was averted when a sudden gale blew up and drove the enemy ships out to sea. No doubt the citizens breathed a sigh of relief at their good fortune, but was it nature or Divine Providence following a prayer offered by the Revd Robert Shirra, a Kirkcaldy minister, that prevented the attack?

Several stories have been related regarding that memorable incident: that Mr Shirra took an old chair to the beach where he sat and prayed, vowing that if God did not answer his prayers and raise a storm to drive the privateers away from the coast, he would remain there until the tide came in and he drowned; or did he go to the water's edge, where, accompanied by a large terror-stricken congregation, he fell on his knees and asked for deliverance?

The most likely explanation is that the minister, seeing a crowd watching the ships, called at the home of one of his congregation and asked what was causing all the excitement. On being told that the ships in the distance were American privateers Mr Shirra allegedly prayed: 'Lord, if they are enemies, put thou a hook in their nose and a bridle in their jaw and take them back to where they came from'.

Shortly afterwards Mr Shirra made his way to the shore to witness the spectacle, where, it is said, he remarked to a friend: 'The Lord wi' His wind could easily blaw them out of the Firth'.

Whether by faith or good fortune the gale rose, and Jones's ships were blown out to sea never to return.

Jones was the son of a Kirkcudbright gardener and was born in 1747. Curiously he had a Leith connection, for it was believed that his grandfather kept a 'mail-garden' or 'public', better known today as a market garden, in Leith. The villain of the piece was born John Paul on 7 July 1747, in a cottage overlooking the Solway Firth. It was not until 1773 that he adopted the name Paul Jones. At the age of 12 he was apprenticed to a shipowner in Whitehaven. Paul served on the slaver *King George* and by his nineteenth year he was mate on another slaver — *The Two Friends*. During the period 1769–70 he commanded the merchantman *John* and made two trips to the West Indies. While in Tobago on the second voyage he allegedly flogged the carpenter, Mungo Maxwell, for neglect of duty, and several weeks later Maxwell died at sea. Maxwell's father had Paul charged with murder but he was released from prison on bail, and while awaiting trial he obtained sworn statements establishing his innocence. In 1773 John Paul was again in Tobago as master of *The Betesey* of London.

The crew mutinied, and in an incident that followed, the ringleader died from wounds received from a sword held by the master. Paul alleged that the victim died when he ran on to the sword! On this occasion, however, there were witnesses who were prepared to give evidence against Paul and he fled to America. It was at this time he changed his name, in all probability to conceal his true identity. He was commissioned in the American navy in 1775 where his outstanding seamanship was quickly recognised and promotion was rapid.

In 1777 Jones was posted to Europe and in April of the following year he sailed from Brest for the Irish Sea. He attacked Whitehaven, and, after spiking the town's guns he attempted to set fire to the shipping. He planned also to take the Earl of Selkirk as a hostage to ensure the proper treatment of American prisoners. His intended victim was not at home, but the crew did not go empty-handed, taking a quantity of silver. He returned to Brest after 28 days with a sizeable quantity of booty, including seven vessels and a number of prisoners. His activities had caused considerable concern in Britain where Jones's reputation as corsair was much respected.

The pirate was then given command of the French ship *Duras* which he promptly renamed *Bon Homage Richard*. On 14 August 1779, Jones again put to sea, this time paying particular attention to the east coast. He was supported by and *Vengeance* and *Pallas*.

Jones, who had now attained the rank of Commodore, described his exploits in a report dated 3 October 1779 to

Benjamin Franklin who was the American Ambassador to France at the time Jones was active in British waters. He wrote:

> The winds continued to be contrary, so that we did not see the land till the 13th. (September) when the hills of Cheviot, in the south-east of Scotland, appeared. The next day we chased sundry vessels, and took a ship and a brigantine, both from the Frith of Edinburgh, laden with coal. Knowing that there lay at anchor in Leith Roads an armed ship of 20 guns, with two or three fine cutters, I formed an expedition against Leith, which I purposed to lay under contribution, or otherwise to reduce it to ashes. Had I been alone, the wind being favourable, I would have proceeded directly up the Frith and must have succeeded, as they lay then in a state of perfect indolence and security, which would have proved their ruin. Unfortunately for me, the *Pallas* and *Vengeance* were both at a considerable distance in the offing, they having chased to the southward. This obliged me to steer out of the Frith again to meet them. The captains of the *Pallas* and *Vengeance* being come on board the *Bon Homme Richard*, I communicated to them my project, to which many difficulties and objections were made by them. At last, however, they appeared to think better of the design, after I had assured them that I hoped to raise a contribution of £200,000 sterling on Leith, and that there was no battery of cannon there to oppose our landing. So much time, however, was unavoidably spent in pointed remarks and sage deliberations that night, that the wind became contrary in the morning.

On 15 September the three privateers were spotted off Eyemouth, and later in the day, at Dunbar, about seven miles out to sea. Next day the progress was being watched by the citizens of Leith and Edinburgh. By 5 p.m. the ships were clearly visible. Next day they had taken positions opposite Kirkcaldy with the *Bon Homme Richard's* broadside facing the town.

Meanwhile the townfolk of Leith worked feverishly to repel the expected attack. A number of old cannons with their carriages, and in a very poor state, were man-handled from the Timber Bush over the old stone bridge at the Coalhill, to be mounted on the ruined citadel. A few brass field-pieces manned by artillery-men, were stationed at Newhaven and the incorporation of traders petitioned the Commander-in-Chief at Edinburgh Castle for arms which were readily supplied. Even sacks of wool were requisitioned to build barricades, and all night long, soldiers and seamen patrolled the front.

Such was Jones's confidence that at one time he was almost within cannon range of the town, but this was no foolhardy act, for the attacker was well aware of the defenceless state of Leith. This information had been provided by Andrew Robertson of Kirkcaldy, whose vessel the *Friendship* had been taken by Jones. In return for this service the pirate had agreed to release Robertson and his boat.

Jones's intention had been to press home an immediate attack on the port, but his two support ships were still some way to the south. He decided to sail out of the Forth, to rendezvous with them. Vital time was squandered, however; the wind rose and the initiative was lost.

In anticipation of his success this Scottish-American had prepared the following letter which he had intended to have delivered to Leith Town Council. It was from: 'The Honourable J. Paul Jones, Commander-in-Chief of the American Squadron now in Europe, etc., to the Worshipful the Provost of Leith, or, in his absence, to the Chief Magistrate who is now actually present and in authority there'.

> Sir, The British marine force that has been stationed here for the protection of your city and commerce being now taken by the American arms under my command, I have the honour to send you this summons by my officer, Lieutenant-Colonel de Chamillard who commands the vanguard of my troops. I do not wish to distress the poor inhabitants; my intention is only to demand your contribution towards the reimbursement which Britain owes to the much injured citizens of the United States — for savages would blush at the unmanly violation and rapacity that has marked the tracks of British tyranny in America, from which neither virgin innocence nor hapless age has been a plea for protection or pity. Leith and its port now lies at our mercy; and did not our humanity stay the hand of just retaliation, I should, without advertisement, lay it in ashes.
> Before I proceed to that stern duty as an officer, my duty as a man induces me to propose to you, by the means of a reasonable ransom, to prevent such a scene of horror and distress. For this reason I have authorised Lieutenant-Colonel de Chamillard to conclude and agree with you on the terms of ransom, allowing you exactly half-an-hour's reflection before you finally accept or reject the terms which he shall propose (£200,000). If you accept the terms offered within the time limited, you may rest assured that no further debarkation of troops will be made, but that the re-embarkation of the vanguard will

immediately follow, and that the property of the citizens will remain unmolested. I have the honour to be, with sentiments of due respect, Sir, your very obedient and very humble servant, Paul Jones. On board the American ship-of-war the *Bon Homme Richard*, at anchor in the Road of Leith, September the 17th, 1779.

The letter was never dispatched.

– 11 –
THE THEATRE ROYAL...
AND AN ILL FATED SITE

Travellers crossing the North Bridge in the late 18th century would have made their first contact with the New Town in the vicinity of Shakespeare Square, which stood on the site of the GPO building. It was certainly not one of the most attractive of Edinburgh's squares, and, completed in 1778, consisted of shops, lodging houses and a theatre — the Theatre Royal. Architecturally this building had little to recommend it. One 19th-century writer described this edifice as 'one of the plainest and most commonplace buildings in the city and were it not for its colonnade front, erected by Mr. Murray in 1830, it might have been mistaken for a granary or barn'. Internally, however, the theatre was described as being elegantly fitted. Above the entrance was a statue of Shakespeare with figures depicting Tragic and Comic muse. The hall had cost £5,000 to construct and was opened in December 1769. While its appearance may not have been particularly appealing, it gave Edinburgh audiences the opportunity to see the best of the London performers.

When it opened the admission charges were: boxes and pits, three shillings; lower gallery, two shillings; second and upper galleries, one shilling. 'Takings' amounted to approximately £140 a night. On 21 September 1854 came the news that the theatre and adjoining properties had been acquired for the GPO building. Demolition followed, and on 23 September 1861 Prince Albert laid the foundation stone and work was completed five years later.

Destroyed by Fire

The site at the corner of Broughton Street and Little King Street had long been associated with buildings that provided entertainment. It was also a location plagued by misfortune, and all five theatres which were built on this site were destroyed by fire — four of them were named the Theatre Royal. As far back as 1789 a lease was entered into between Walter Ferguson, writer, and Robert Inglis, mason, in respect of this location. After several

The Theatre Royal, Shakespeare Square.

transactions it was acquired by Natali Corri, a dealer in music and musical instruments, who converted the amphitheatre on the site into concert rooms and then a theatre. It was known as the Pantheon, later the Caledonian, and finally the Adelphi. This theatre was managed by Robert Henry Wyndham who was well-known in the theatrical business and had made appearances at the Theatre Royal, Shakespeare Square.

On 24 May 1853 the Adelphi was destroyed in a fire, causing damage to St Mary's RC chapel (it had not yet attained Cathedral status). The outbreak was discovered at approximately 4.45 p.m., and the flames spread so rapidly that within an hour only the four walls remained. It reopened on 19 December 1855 as the Queen's Theatre and Opera House under Wyndham's management. When the Theatre Royal, Shakespeare Square closed, the 'Queen's' adopted the title. Thereafter followed a bizarre sequence of disasters when, over a period of 81 years, four theatres on this location, all named the Theatre Royal, were destroyed by fire.

By far the worst conflagration struck on Friday 13 January 1865, resulting in the deaths of six people. This was the only occasion in the history of the theatre on which there were fatalities, as fortunately all the fires occurred when the premises were closed to performances, otherwise the consequences would have been catastrophic.

The time was approaching 4 p.m. on that fateful day and the staff were completing their preparations for the evening performance of the pantomime *Little Tom Tucker*. Cassey, the theatre gas-man, was lighting the rows of gas jets which were attached to the 'borders' (strips of painted canvas which stretched across the tops of the scenery to hide the back-stage from the audience). These lights were required to illuminate the stage, and it was a routine which Cassey had carried out frequently. With quick efficiency he lit the back row and was in the process of attending to the jets located in front when the border caught fire. It was not the first time this had happened, and Cassey was not particularly worried, as the problem had been solved by removing the canvas to prevent it spreading the flames. This time, however, the outbreak was more severe and the gas-man rushed along the 'flies' (wooden platforms which were used by the staff when moving scenery) at the same time yelling for the assistance of Syme (fireman), Stewart (head carpenter) and Glen (general assistant); but his pleas for help went unanswered. Why? Because members of the staff had on a number of occasions raised false alarms, and the fireman may have assumed that it was another practical joke. Perhaps, of course, the call was never heard. Had Syme responded immediately to the call for assistance, the theatre may have been saved and also the lives of six men.

Cassey traced Syme to the carpenters' workshop and explained the problem to him; but already precious minutes had been lost. The staff immediately rushed to where the fire was now raging, intending to cut the scenery support ropes, thus dropping the canvas backing and stamping out the fire. But luck was not on Syme's side on that Friday the thirteenth. Apparently in his rush to investigate he had dropped his knife — and none of the others had one. A hose was then put to use but by now the situation was beyond their control and the men had no option but to abandon the building and raise the alarm.

R.H. Wyndham, who was lessee of the theatre, was in London. His wife had left the premises at 3.30 p.m. to visit her daughter in Ainslie Place and learned of the outbreak as she made her way back to the Theatre Royal. Her brothers, Edward and Richard Sacker, were walking in Princes Street when a pedestrian gave them the news. They rushed back to discover that the back entrance was already inaccessible. But by using a ladder they reached the wardrobe room, located at the front, overlooking Broughton Street and immediately above a spirit-dealer's shop. As a result of their efforts a large quantity of valuable silk, velvet and satin dresses and other props were saved. As these items were thrown from broken windows, members of the public bundled them into cabs and then had them removed to a temporary store.

The interior of the theatre was soon consumed but none of the local residents were aware of the disaster until the flames had burst through the roof. As the fire continued unabated, people in various parts of the town noticed a glow which lit up the winter evening sky and spectators were soon causing congestion in the vicinity of the theatre. Not until 4.30 p.m. was the first hose playing on the Theatre Royal building but it was already obvious that there was no chance of preventing total destruction. The decision was then taken to ensure the safety of the adjoining residential property. Fifteen minutes after the arrival of the fire-fighters the theatre roof collapsed and the flames continued relentlessly. The noise was described as 'like that of a mighty furnace'. Worse was to follow when it was discovered that the attics of the line of houses immediately adjacent to the Little King Street side of the theatre were alight. There was no delay as the residents set about salvaging their possessions. Soon the flats on the opposite side of the street were similarly affected and rafters and joists could be seen burning furiously. Spectators willingly joined in the rescue operations, carrying some of the bigger household items downstairs. Soft furnishings were thrown from windows, often to the surprise of those below. As more engines arrived all efforts were concentrated on protecting living accommodation. This was eventually achieved but not without sacrifice. Fire damaged the upper structures and lower properties suffered badly from the effects of water.

By 5 p.m. the number of spectators had grown to such an extent that three officers and 250 men were brought from the castle to undertake crowd control.

As the afternoon turned into early evening two engines and 80 men arrived from Leith to offer assistance. There was a problem, however, for the water pressure could not meet the demand. A decision was taken to withdraw the Leith Dock Commission engine, leaving the artillery men from Leith Fort to carry on. Fifty Leith policemen were also on the scene, providing valuable assistance.

The situation became critical at about 6 p.m. when the authorities became concerned at the structural state of the north wall of the theatre which was leaning outwards. St Mary's church was the adjacent property and it had been evident for an hour that the wall was in danger of collapse. After several warnings there was a sharp crack; the wall split in two and crashed through the roof of the cloisters. Damage to the church was considerable. To the west of the chapel was a dwellinghouse for the clergy, extending north from the wall of the theatre to a narrow lane (Cathedral Lane) leading from St James Place to Broughton Street. Shortly after 4 p.m., when the severity of the fire was evident, Bishop Strain, assisted by four priests, removed all paintings and other valuables from the church and house. These included the large well-known picture showing the entombment of the Saviour which had been located immediately above the altar. Shortly after 5 p.m. a chimney-stalk fell from the theatre onto the cupola of the cloister and into the vestry. There were two men in the vestry and rescuers immediately rushed to their assistance. One was dead; the second was alive but jammed against a wall and crying piteously for help.

Among those present was Lord Dean of Guild George Lorimer, a much respected businessman in the town. He had been present for most of the duration of the fire and immediately became actively involved in the efforts to rescue the injured man. While they worked frantically in dangerous conditions Lorimer and his colleagues were warned that the north wall was in danger of collapsing but they persisted in their efforts to free the trapped man. Some heeded what they were told, left the building and lived — others died in the frantic efforts to save a life, as the wall finally caved outwards. Shortly afterwards, and when it was considered safe, a team of rescuers went into the debris in a forlorn hope of finding someone alive. After 90 minutes they found the body of a man. He was in a sitting position and was later identified as George Sweeney, aged 67, a butler who lived at 15 Leopold Place. He left a widow and a grown-up family of four. One hour later the remains of John Clark, aged 66, 4 Middle Arthur Place, were located in the rubble. A widow and adult family of seven were left to grieve. Ironically John Clark had spent 40 years in the fire service in Edinburgh and for much of that time he had been Captain of the Fountainbridge detachment. He had been retired for only a few months.

A 26-year-old clerk, Thomas Henry Leeke, was found dead a few minutes later. He had gone to the church to help in saving the pictures and was trapped when the chimney stalk collapsed. It was while efforts were underway to rescue him that the theatre wall collapsed. His widow and daughter, aged seven, lived at 51 Broughton Street. By 3 a.m. on Saturday only three bodies had been recovered. The only good news was that the fire was out — there was nothing left that was combustible. After another couple of hours of searching the bodies of two victims were located lying side-by-side, but a considerable distance from where the other bodies had been found, suggesting that the two heroes had made a late frantic but unsuccessful attempt to run for safety as the wall gave way. It was quickly established that they were the remains of John Taylor, believed to have been 55 years of age, who worked as a stonemason and had lived at 4 St James Square with his wife, a 16-year-old daughter and sons aged 14 and seven respectively; and George Lorimer who was 54 and resided at Mayfield Terrace. He was survived by his widow and a family of four. John Taylor was no stranger to danger. On 24 November 1861 he had been involved in rescue work during the 'Heave Awa" tenement collapse in the High Street when 35 people died.

At 7 a.m. the body of the last victim was removed from the building. It was that of Bernard McVie of Baxter's Close, Lawnmarket, aged 54, married, with six children whose ages ranged from five to seventeen.

Damage to the theatre was complete; St Mary's and the priests' house was considerable; one-third of the chapel had been destroyed. The pulpit, which was located adjacent to the wall of the theatre was relatively undamaged although heaps of masonry had fallen all around it. Also destroyed were railings in front of the altar and the altar steps.

Examination of the remains of the theatre walls confirmed that they were in danger of further collapse, and the site was barricaded while demolition work was carried out. The church could not be used for services, and arrangements were made for the congregation to attend St Patrick's, Cowgate, at 10 a.m. and noon.

This was to continue until St Mary's had been brought back into a useable state.

Three of the victims were buried on the Tuesday following the fire. George Sweeney was laid to rest at the Grange cemetery, following a service at his home which commenced at 2 p.m. Half-an-hour later Thomas Leeke's remains were taken to Warriston cemetery. The mourners included uniformed members of No. 8 Battery of the City of Edinburgh Artillery Volunteers. Mr Leeke had been a serving sergeant. Then at 3 p.m. the body of John Clark left his son's house in Middle Arthur Place for the Grange cemetery where there was a big turnout of Fire Brigade representatives. It was the following day before the remains of John Taylor were taken to Warriston cemetery. The whereabouts of the resting place of Bernard McVie are, to me, unknown.

The funeral of Lord Dean of Guild George Lorimer also took place on Wednesday. This was an impressive occasion and in many respects resembled a miniature military funeral. George Lorimer's family home was in Mayfield Terrace, and prior to burial in St Cuthbert's graveyard a service was held at his house.

It was conducted jointly by the Revd J.C. Cumming, minister at Newington church (where Mr Lorimer was an Elder) and the Revd Dr Paul of St Cuthbert's. Simultaneously the Revd Maxwell Nicholson held a service at Newington church in Clerk Street, for the benefit of the representatives of the public organisations who were later to join the funeral procession. At 1 p.m. the bells of Newington and St Cuthtert's began to peal and they continued until the committal had been completed.

The cortege was taken by way of Blacket Place and at this stage the procession was led by the High Constables with the insignia of office draped in crape, followed by a line of carriages. Immediately behind the Lord Provost's coach, which carried Bailies Cassels and Alexander, came the hearse drawn by four horses. To the rear of the hearse were 20 carriages occupied by relatives and friends, then 40 private vehicles.

The cortège left Newington church, led by eight police constables who marched four abreast. They were followed by the representatives of many public organisations; Masonic Lodge Journeymen No. 8; Directors of the Western Cemetery; Provost and Magistrates of Leith; High School Club; Rector and Masters of the High School, Chamber of Commerce; Merchant Company;

Incorporation of Guildry; City Road Trust; Lord Advocate; Dean of Guild Court; Society of High Constables; City Officers with halberts craped; sword and mace bearers with the insignia draped with crape, Council Officer; Town Council and officials; City Clerk; Treasurer, Convenor, and Magistrates. As they moved off the mourners who had attended the service at the Lord Dean's home took up positions to the rear. The procession stretched for three-quarters of a mile.

It was a typical dismal Edinburgh January day and heavy rain fell for most of the afternoon. Nevertheless, the citizens turned out in large numbers to line the streets and pay their homage, and the shops closed. As the cortège approached the corner of the North Bridge and Princes Street the construction men working on the GPO building stood cap in hand and eyes to the ground in silent respect — not a surprising gesture, for George Lorimer was respected by all in the building industry. He was recognised by the men as one of the best of employers, and to those men 'he extended both his hand and his purse while they were in distress or difficulty'.

Among those at the graveside were Bishop Strain and other members of the clergy from St Mary's, Mr Wyndham, and most of the male members of the cast. An hour had elapsed since the remains of Lorimer had left his home. The coffin was carried by the Master and five Past-Masters of the Masonic Lodge Journeymen No. 8. The walk was lined by the High Constables, and members of the town council and magistrates joined the family at the graveside. But there is one mystery — where was George Lorimer buried?

A contemporary account of the committal ceremony is quite specific: 'The lamented Dean was buried in the family ground adjoining the wall next to Castle Terrace [in fact King's Stables Road] beside his father and mother, two brothers and two sisters, the dates of whose deaths are recorded on a handsome tablet at the head of the grave'. There is one George Lorimer named on this stone, and he died, aged 52, on 1 September 1833 — 32 years before the Theatre Royal fire, and this obviously refers to the father.

Close to the church door which faces Princes Street, however, there is another Lorimer stone which includes the inscription: 'In memory of George Lorimer born 17 January 1812, died 13 January

1865', which is the date of the Theatre Royal fire. Reports at the time gave his age as 53, and the details on this stone indicate that George Lorimer was in his fifty-third year at the time of his death. Perhaps George Lorimer was buried beside his parents, and for some inexplicable reason his name was never recorded. There is certainly enough space on the gravestone for his details to be inscribed.

The tablet near the church does give full details of this branch of the family; was the name of George Lorimer, Lord Dean of Guild, included as a memorial rather than to mark his resting place?

Once More (1875)

A new Theatre Royal rose from the ashes and was completed in 1866 at a cost of £17,000. In 1874 the theatre was sold for £11,000 but within a year disaster struck once more and destruction was swift. Only half-an-hour after the fire had been discovered at 2 p.m. on Saturday 6 February 1875 the building was a blazing inferno, and by 4 p.m. only the four walls remained. At the time of the outbreak there were few people on the premises. Mrs Fraser and two assistants were busy in the wardrobe room working on dresses for the current show, the pantomime *Jack in the Beanstalk*, and a cashier occupied the box-office which was located in the entrance.

Shortly before the fire, the cast had assembled in a room, known as the treasury, to be paid their salaries. Others were wandering about the stage. Smoking was banned, and this rule was strictly observed by staff and cast. At this time there was no evidence of the disaster that was about to strike.

It was approximately 2.05 p.m. when Mrs Fraser became aware of a rush of air through the room. At the same time there was a loud noise coming from the vicinity of the gas-room which was located at the opposite side of the stage. The box-office assistant was startled when the inner glass doors swung outwards, caused apparently, by a gust of wind so strong that pictures were blown from the walls onto the floor. Those on duty immediately left the theatre, but already black smoke was pouring through the roof over the stage. Within minutes part of the roof had been destroyed and there was great concern for the safety of nearby flats which were located in tenements six and seven storeys high. In Little King Street blistering was noticed on the wooden window frames which were in danger of catching fire. Instructions were given that these flats were to be evacuated and this duty was carried out by Sergeant Crawford (who had been on duty at the previous fire) and a team of constables.

The first fire-fighters on the scene were from the Central firestation and Rose Street. They immediately concentrated on the south and west walls of the theatre, but shortly afterwards the firemen were re-deployed to protect the residents in Little King Street where windows on both sides were alight. Bit by bit the theatre building gave way, and when the steam engine arrived at 2.45 p.m. the fire was at its height. The presence of this vehicle added another three hoses to the firefighters' efforts. For a time water was poured onto the roof of the Cloister chapel St Mary's in an effort to hold back the flames, and, when it was believed that the church building was secure, attention was turned to the north wall of the theatre which was sloping outwards. The wall was monitored with fearful anxiety for it was the corresponding wall in the former theatre which had collapsed in 1865 resulting in the loss of life. When the theatre had been rebuilt iron rods were inserted to strengthen the structure. It was now under test.

The front of the theatre remained intact and this was attributed to the design, which included a brick wall erected between the auditorium and the entrance. Meanwhile, on the south side, in Little King Street, flames continued to shoot through window openings and the large door used for the movement of scenery. There was reason to believe that this wall was in danger of collapse, and a hose was taken up Little King Street and fed in through the scenery door, while a small engine at the top of the street continued to play an important part in the operation. A six-storey tenement to the south of the burning theatre was now under threat but prompt action soon had this out-break under control. As a precaution, however, firemen continued to play water on the roof to ensure that it remained wet and cool.

The scene was graphically recorded in a contemporary report:

By and by a fireman appeared, hose in hand, on the very top of the chimney-stack overlooking a burning area and very picturesque he looked. The glare of the flames below was reflected from the brass helmet and he stood out in statuesque relief against the grey lowering sky. The object which secured such an excellent picture was, however, not so obvious, for the jet of water which the man threw towards the fire-lake below must have been as ineffectual as a streamlet turned on Vesuvius in eruption. Long before the water could have reached the flames it must have been converted into steam and carried away heavenwards.

Just when it seamed that the situation was under control a new crisis arose. In a shop near the entrance to the stalls, there was a large stock of whisky which was valued by the owner at £1,000, although insured for only £400. Flames were now moving eastwards, and if they reached the shop, an explosion was inevitable. The fire authorities were aware of the problem and when, about 3.30 p.m., flames had penetrated the partition wall, a hose was diverted from another area and the situation brought under control. Within half-an-hour, however, flames gained hold at the north-east corner of the roof, and spreading, again caused a potential threat to the whisky stock. Immediately a quick-thinking fireman placed a ladder near the window, smashed the glass and directed the hose to the danger area. The spirit was saved

Shortly before 4 p.m. the conflagration had reached the semicircular partition which separated the entrance corridors and passageways from the interior. Soon all was devoured and with nothing between the street and the interior, the devastation was all too evident. From time to time the flames would rise, but there were a dozen hoses at the ready to douse any further threats. At the express request of the Lord Provost further assistance was requested from Leith, and within a short time a further engine was in action. Not surprisingly, and considering the history of this site, the fire attracted a large number of spectators, and the 1st Battalion, Royal Scots, were summoned from the castle to restore some order; this was achieved, but only with difficulty. As the time approached 5.30 p.m. the Leith Dock's fire-fighting equipment had also arrived, but by now it was too late — the Theatre Royal had been gutted, and all that could be done was to concentrate water on glowing embers, the walls of the church, and nearby residential properties. In the meantime work had started on barricading the devastated area and that was completed by 10 p.m.

It was a particularly sad occasion for R.H. Wyndham who had managed three theatres on this location — and all had been destroyed by fire. The popular and successful pantomime *Jack in the Beanstalk* had only two weeks to run. The expenditure on this show was £2,000 and Wyndham had planned to stage opera followed by a new production of *Rob Roy* (on which a considerable amount had been spent on 'props') to mark the end of his career at the Theatre Royal.

Among the many items destroyed were manuscripts and marked editions of plays which had been given to Wyndham by the widow of the famous Eton-educated actor, Charles Kean, who died in 1868. The leader of the orchestra, Mr Daly, had left a violin valued at £50 on the premises. Unfortunately he did not even own the instrument which he had on loan. Sadly, the fire also meant that a considerable number of actors and theatre employees were out of work.

An investigation of the ruins on the Monday following the fire failed to establish the cause of the outbreak, but it was believed that it had started in the lighting above the stage.

Yet Again (1884)

Little time was wasted in replacing the Theatre Royal and the site was sold for £5,000 following the fire. A new structure was designed and construction work completed in three months, at a cost of £12,500. The hall had a capacity of 2,300 and opened on 27 January 1876 with a performance of Boncicault's *Shaughraun*.

There were advantages in living in Little King Street. It was in the centre of the town with access to a plentiful supply of shops and rents were relatively cheap as reflected in the large number of poorer families who occupied these tenements. But this was also a street where tenancies were accepted with a certain amount of trepidation. The Theatre Royal was constantly in the minds of the locals because of its close proximity to the houses and its reputation for being fire-prone, and the year 1884 was no exception.

Only nine years had elapsed since the building had been gutted, when disaster struck again. Such was the intensity of the heat that attic flats in Little King Street caught fire and flames spread to the roof of the Cathedral and the Archbishop's residence. Fortunately there was no loss of life.

Experience had shown that previous outbreaks had started in the vicinity of the stage, but on this occasion the seat of the blaze was immediately above the entrance. In less than two hours the Theatre Royal had been consumed.

The Theatre Royal and St Mary's Cathedral, photographed at the beginning of the 20th century (Reproduced by kind permission of the Administrator, St Mary's Cathedral).

The alarm was raised about noon on 30 June 1884 by Mr Paterson, a bookseller at 15 Broughton Street who was walking in the vicinity and noticed a smell of burning and black smoke in the vicinity of the theatre. He immediately informed the St James police-station before returning to the theatre, and he alerted Peter Crabb, a member of the staff, who was about to leave the building. He immediately rushed to the area identified by Paterson which was a 'props' room, measuring 20 feet by 12 feet. By this time the flames were spreading to a corridor behind the gallery.

Unbelievably a company were on stage rehearsing a drama entitled *The Nightingale* which would have had its first performance that night. While Crabb turned off the gas an actor played a hose onto the now burning woodwork, but to no avail. The fire spread quickly, consuming the refreshment bar, the workshops and the entrance to the gallery. In no time it spread along the roof and finally reached a sunlight window. Fortunately many of the company's effects were saved, including live rabbits and birds which were required in the production.

The fire brigade were soon on the scene with a force of between 25 and 30 men. It was quickly established that the fire had penetrated the roof above the entrance and the theatre was now beyond being saved. A decision was taken to move the equipment to St James Place, behind the theatre, and hoses were taken into the building from this location. But such was the relentless progress of the conflagration that the firemen were forced to withdraw.

As might be expected on such occasions, spectators were now arriving in large numbers, and at one time consideration was given to calling in the troops to exercise control, but a joint effort by the police, High Constables and councillors soon restored order. The fight to save the Theatre Royal continued, and while one unit concentrated on the rear section a second detachment laid hoses from the front to the gallery and the second circle. There was concern about the north wall, and the water supply from St James Place and Little King Street had insufficient pressure to reach the roof. The problem was further compounded because new water pipes were being laid in front of the theatre where a four-inch was being replaced by a five-inch bore. But the quick-thinking foreman in charge of the pipe-laying gang had anticipated the situation and had made a temporary supply available. The fire-fighters also had access to a hydrant opposite St Mary's and a 12-inch main in York Place. With the blaze now out of control, assistance was required from Leith but in reality it was too late.

For a time the flames were prevented from reaching the entrance hall to the dress circle, which enabled staff to rescue pictures which had decorated this once fine theatre. The adjoining tobacconist's shop was, however, destroyed, with the loss of stock valued at £200.

Within an hour of the alarm being raised, there was concern for the safety of all the surrounding buildings. The theatre roof was burning furiously and at the stage end there was a large seven-storey tenement which at one time was feared would be destroyed. The windows were open and at all of them the faces of anxious tenants could be seen, trying to calculate when it would be necessary to start throwing soft furnishings to the street below. On the theatre side of the street, the tenements, six storeys high, were in even greater danger. Here, in sub-divided flats, lived some of the poorest people. These families (40 of them) made every effort to save their precious belongings by throwing water onto the wooden window frames, and the flats at the lower levels were secured. The heat eventually became so overpowering that the

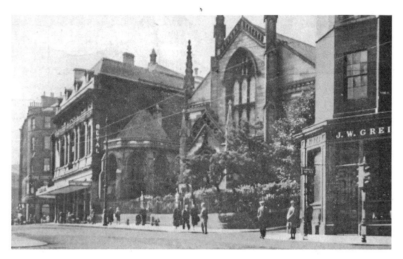

This view was probably taken in the mid-1930s, after the theatre had undergone major refurbishment. The pillars had been removed and a modern canopy erected. To the left, the tenements of Little King Street; on the right, a traffic signal — the first in Edinburgh — erected at the junction of York Place and Broughton Street, and operational on 21 March 1928. (Reproduced by kinds permission of the Administrator, St Mary's Cathedral).

attic properties had to be abandoned and left to their fate. On several roofs the lead melted and ran down the outer walls. By this time the firemen were being hampered by the loss of water pressure and premises above the second level could not be reached; but the problem was soon overcome and efforts continued to save the residential properties.

There was sadness for many of the residents. What the flames had failed to destroy was considerably damaged by water. The Miles family, husband, wife and three children occupied a single attic room. Mr Miles had been unemployed for seven months but had recently found a job. Now he had lost everything. Many of the families were not covered by insurance. For a time a large tenement in St James Place was in danger and many of the families, no doubt aware of previous outbreaks, took the precaution of removing household items to the opposite side of the street. A change in wind direction saved the situation.

Meanwhile, a great deal of attention was being paid to St Mary's Cathedral, and the roof of the servants' quarter at the Archbishop's residence caught fire. Quick action by the residents soon extinguished the flames. At the height of the outbreak the heat was of such intensity that the shutters across the way, at 30 Greenside Street, were badly blistered. Number 2 Little King Street was similarly affected and the paintwork was described as being 'peeled off as if a hot iron had been applied to it'.

In the year prior to this fire a great deal of money had been spent on the theatre, the interior having been painted throughout and expensive decorations provided for the dress circle, private boxes and adjacent corridors. In the week preceding the latest catastrophe, the famous French actress, Sarah Bernhardt, had appeared on the Monday and Tuesday. She died as recently as 1923. The remainder of the week had been taken up by the Majilton company in *Round the Clock,* prior to the opening of *The Nightingale.*

And Finally (1946)

The end for the Theatre Royal came on the night of Saturday 30 March 1946, when it was gutted in what was described as one of the fiercest blazes in Edinburgh for a considerable period. It was not an old theatre, having been completely refurbished only ten years previously. In a few hours much of the structure had been destroyed and the cost of damage was estimated at £75,000.

Minutes before the outbreak was discovered, Tommy Morgan and his cast had played to a packed audience watching the very popular *Hail Caledonia* show. By 10.40 p.m. the last of the public had been ushered from the hall and only a handful of staff remained — the assistant manager, night watchman, usherettes and cleaners. The outbreak started in the gallery 35 minutes later. The alarm was raised by the watchman, and the first fire-engine arrived within two minutes, but despite the efforts of units from London Road, Leith, Victoria Dock, Musselburgh and Dalkeith, they were unable to save this popular theatre.

Two turn-table ladders were in use and searchlights were played on the building to assist the firefighters. At one stage the flames were shooting 40 feet into the air and the conflagration spread rapidly. Around midnight the roof collapsed. As a precaution, families living in the vicinity were evacuated and were provided with temporary accommodation in church halls located in St James Place.

Assistant manager Peter Robertson was in the office when, about 11.15 p.m., a cleaner reported seeing smoke circulating in the gallery. The watchman, William Fraser (aged 56) investigated, called the fire brigade and calmly played a hose on the flames until the professionals arrived shortly afterwards. Fortunately the fire safety screen had been dropped immediately after the performance and although part of the stage and scenery were damaged, the dressing-rooms, workshops and 'props' were relatively unaffected. About midnight the flames burst through the roof and it was not long before large sections of timbers crashed into the pits, causing the fire to spread rapidly. An hour later the fire was all but out, although firemen remained on duty throughout Sunday as a precaution. All day the site was visited by countless numbers of citizens. Many were regular theatregoers who each week had paid a few shillings to see the current show and, for a few hours had watched such household names as Harry Gordon, Dave Willis, Jack Anthony, Tommy Lorne and Will Fyffe.

The property owners were confident that the Theatre Royal would be rebuilt and a figure of £100,000 had been quoted. It was hoped that work would start at an early date and open by the end of the year. Unfortunately these optimistic views were not shared by the authorities.

It was the immediate post-war period, building materials were in short supply, and there were many projects such as housing which carried a greater degree of priority.

At a meeting of the Streets and Building Committee held at the City Chambers on 5 June 1947, the Town Clerk reminded the councillors that a special sub-committee had met in December 1946, when the question of obtaining an alternative theatre site had been discussed. The owners had subsequently informed the Council that they preferred the existing location, as they were more hopeful of obtaining a Ministry of Works licence to rebuild the ruined structure than for new work. After much discussion the committee signified their approval, but it was close and went in favour of the applicants, Edinburgh Varieties Ltd, on the casting vote of the chairman — and was subject to the approval of the Town Council.

One week later the full Council decided on a vote of 40–13 to continue consideration of the matter. A new Theatre Royal was now becoming a controversial subject and E.G. Willis, MP. for

Edinburgh North, expressed his concern in the House of Commons that a licence had been granted when houses were so desperately needed.

In July 1947 the Town Council indicated that they were not opposed to the replacement of the theatre, but believed that it must form part of a major redevelopment involving an area bounded by St James Square, York Place, Calton Hill and the top of Leith Walk — and the work would have to be carried out in stages.

The matter dragged on and the owners appealed to the Secretary of State against the refusal of the Council to grant consent to replace the theatre. On 17 September 1948 this appeal was dismissed. The Secretary of State had taken the view that reconstruction on the same site would prejudice the redevelopment of the area as a whole. In issuing his decision, however, the Secretary of State said that he regarded the provision of a new theatre in this area as desirable in the public interest and he indicated to the Corporation that he would be glad if they took steps to make a new site available as soon as possible. On 3 November 1950 the Council, by a majority of 36–13 resolved to grant consent for a limited period of thirty years.

Two years later it was reported that work would commence 'in a few months time'. But that was subject to obtaining a Ministry of Works licence and the Ministry made it clear that the restoration of the Theatre Royal was automatically ruled out by the ban on building work costing more than £5,000 which applied to any place of entertainment. No promise had been given regarding the issue of a licence but they indicated that the Ministry would keep the matter in mind. Nevertheless the work involved would have to wait until steel was more readily available and the building materials situation improved. The Ministry indicated that they were sympathetic and aware of the special circumstances relating to the Theatre Royal and the pressure on theatre accommodation caused by the Edinburgh Festival. It was admitted that there was a genuine need in Edinburgh for more theatre space.

In 1953 there were reports that the theatre would reopen the following year. This was immediately denied by the Ministry of Works, who said that no licence had been granted nor had any work been approved in principle.

The saga of the Theatre Royal site dragged on, and in 1954, eight years after the fire, the owners put it on the market. Two

St Mary's Cathedral, which suffered damage frequently from theatre fires. The Theatre Royal was to the left, where the Cathedral extension is now clearly visible.

years later the Town Council considered a proposal to erect a garage and filling station on the land which only ten years previously had 'housed' the Theatre Royal, one of the best known halls in the country. Fortunately the local authority deferred making a decision on the application pending the submission of further details.

Was it the thought of a filling station alongside the Cathedral that prompted the Roman Catholic authorities to act? At a service in St Mary's on 16 December 1956 the congregation were told by Father Patrick Quille that the church had acquired the site of the former theatre 'with a view to further development'. Father Quille added that it was hoped to make the Cathedral worthy of the capital of Scotland and 'we felt we must buy the site of the theatre to make sure the amenity of the Cathedral would be preserved'.

Before any work could commence on the site, however, there was one major social problem. There were ten families living in the tenements which formed part of the acquired land and it would be necessary to find alternative houses for these residents. The purchase would cost the congregation £10,000, and they were already facing a debt of £25,000 in respect of eradicating dry rot in the Cathedral building.

The Theatre Royal/St Mary's Cathedral site has changed beyond all recognition during the post-war era. Major redevelopment has been carried out in the vicinity. After a long battle the remains of the Theatre Royal were demolished, releasing the Cathedral from its previously cramped location, and it now enjoys a broad promenade to the front. Here also are the three major sculptures by Leith-born and locally educated Sir Eduardo Paolozzi. Round the corner, Little King Street remains in name but, thankfully, gone are the high tenements where successive generations of residents lived and nightly heard the reactions of the theatre audiences and lived in constant fear of yet another fire.

– 12 –
'CABIN, DECK AND STEERAGE'

The poor who lived in the once desirable houses of Edinburgh's Old Town must have cast an eye enviously beyond the valley of the former Nor' Loch to where the elegant residences of the affluent and influential citizens were in occupation. Geographically only a short distance separated the two classes but the social gulf was enormous. To the north of the North Bridge were the households where several full-time servants were employed while in the vicinity of the High Street families lived in abject poverty.

Investigative journalism is a much hackneyed phrase in modern newspaper writing but it is not new. In 1866 the *Edinburgh Evening Courant*, prompted by the deplorable standard of housing which existed in the town, carried a series of articles which appeared in that newspaper between 20 October 1866 and 19 January 1867. This exposé shocked and shamed the wealthier classes into action and within a month £100 had been sent to the newspaper for the benefit of the needy families. By modern-day standards this may not seem a great deal of money but 130 years ago it was sufficient to provided 400 families with two bags of coal and 'the remainder of the money has been bestowed in gifts equally beyond the risk of misapplication'. A large selection of warm clothing had also been donated.

There were two schools of thought regarding the improvement of living conditions — one idea was to open new streets through the denser parts of the town, while others believed that the problem could be solved by 'thinning' the more closely-packed and ruinous buildings in these old closes. While the experts argued the poor suffered.

The *Courant* were hard-hitting in their criticism of the ignorance of Edinburgh's rich, regarding the conditions in which the poor suffered. 'Much less is known...of the closes of Edinburgh than of many parts of the interior of Africa; and the internal arrangements of the Red Indian's wigwam are much more familiar to the Christian public than is the condition of the hovels in which many of our towns-people live'.

Practically every house visited in the investigation consisted of a single room, and in some it was impossible for a man of average height, wearing a hat, to stand upright. In several instances, families were discovered living in attics measuring four feet wide, twelve feet long and the height varying between three and six feet. Rents for such facilities were between one and two shillings (five and ten pence) per week paid in advance. Overcrowding was common with families of eight living in one apartment. Facilities regarded as standard in the present-day house were non-existent, and there was no provision for the disposal of rubbish which was kept on landings, behind doors and even under beds until the dust-carts came round.

The *Courant* conceded that it was unreasonable to expect that water and a WC could be provided for each house as many of these flats were not suitable for further conversion, but surely it would be possible to have one well at least, for each court and also receptacles for filth outside the houses. But what must be provided, the newspaper insisted, were houses at rents within the reach of classes who were paying between £3 and £5 a year.

'Is it not possible to erect houses — perhaps of brick — of even a room and closet, with plenty of water, that would give a sufficient return on such rents?' asked the paper.

Among the worst accommodation visited in the course of the investigation was at Crombie's Land, which was located in the middle of the West Port. It was here, just a short time before, that there had been an outbreak of cholera, and the medical practitioners were of the firm view that the buildings should be demolished. Dr Chalmers, the prominent theologian, had long worked for the improvement of housing in this area and shared the views of the medical men that this death-trap should be removed. With this in mind he arranged for a valuation of a house adjacent to the church with the hope of having it cleared from the site and he expected that perhaps in the near future Crombie's Land would also be demolished. A figure of £60 was quoted, but almost immediately the owner raised the figure to £90. This sum the purchaser was prepared to meet, when the asking price was increased to £150, negotiations were abandoned. This was a clear illustration of the problems which those of limited resources had to face in their efforts to improve the lot of the less fortunate members of society.

Crombie's Land had been the cause of great concern to the authorities because of the deplorable state of the 'land'. It was entered through a narrow dirty passage, leading to a small, confined filthy court. The rooms on the first and second storeys were reached by way of rickety stairs and gangways 'remarkable for their dirty condition'.

At the time of the reporter's visit three rooms had been closed to habitation for it was here that eight residents — four from one family —had died from cholera; the disease had simply moved from door to door.

It was estimated that 70 people lived in Crombie's Land, described by Dr Henry Littlejohn, Edinburgh's first Medical Officer of Health, in his report on the sanitary conditions of Edinburgh, as being one of the most overcrowded tenements in the town, and as having been 'built specially for the poor with an eye to a large rental, with small, ill-ventilated rooms, and a great deficiency in sanitary conditions'. A doctor who inspected the building said that he had seen enough 'to convince me that such a place must not only be a hot-bed of disease, but a great and continual nuisance to the locality, both morally and physically'. One flat, measuring ten feet by six feet, was 'home' for four people. When the visitors remarked there was no window, the tenant sarcastically pointed out that there was, drawing their attention to the small opening above the door where glass had been inserted. Rent for this room was one shilling-and-six-pence a week. Despite the dilapidated condition of the building, it was only twenty years old! The proprietor had purchased the ruin for £38. He had added two storeys and was obviously a 19th-century DIY man, having carried out the work 'with my own hand'.

The landlord, a former seaman, described his tenants in the following manner: first floor 'cabin'; second 'deck' and to the rear 'steerage'.

Roofs were built of thin wood covered with layers of metal, believed to have been made from old pots and pans which had been beaten down. These hovels which consisted of 27 rooms, yielded rents of between one-and-six-pence and two shillings (7½ and 10p) a week.

In contrast there was, close by, a block of buildings which illustrated what could be achieved by a caring landlord and co-operative tenants. The structure had been purchased twelve years previously, repaired and let to 30 tenants at rents of less than 2/- (10p) each week. The common passageways and stairs were clean, there were cellars and drying greens to the rear, a water supply to each level and a soil pipe. Accommodation consisted of a room, measuring 18 feet by 13 feet, and a closet, 11 feet by 8 feet. Tenants were required to keep their dwellings and stairs in a clean condition and in return the proprietor agreed to ensure that all repairs were carried out. The stairs were washed twice a week — Wednesday and Saturday — and the owner confirmed that the occupants were well behaved; they took a pride in their homes and when a flat became vacant there were between 20 and 30 applicants.

How, asked the *Courant*, with rents lower than in the worst hovels in the Grassmarket and West Port, was it possible to provide such superior accommodation at lower rents? The proprietor was content with a net return of 10 per cent. Many of the dwellings were beyond saving, and with walls between three and four feet thick, would be difficult to demolish. Surprisingly the point was made that building costs had risen appreciably. Among the reasons given were rises in wages and reduction in working hours in the building industry. It was believed that where possible, restoration would be more economical than demolition. But were wages a major factor in costs? For those residents in work, labouring was the main occupation, and a man could expect to be paid between 12/- and 16/- a week (60p and 80p). Shoemaking and repairing was a popular occupation, although the rewards were small — nine to 14 shillings (45p to 70p) for between 80 and 90 hours a week. Many earned a little money by selling firewood, and this was frequently a family concern. A quantity of wood was purchased for sixpence, broken up, bundled, and sold round the doors. On a good day there would be a profit of fourpence. Some women found work as seamstresses, making mutches (at a penny each) or as washerwomen.

Lack of education was prevalent. Certainly a ragged school had been established by the minister at Greyfriars, and while this had met with some success in the densely populated area around the Grassmarket, this was a task far beyond one man.

Could not George Heriot's Foundation, which has already done so much good in providing education for the children of the better class of working people in the city, be brought to bear to some extent on a class below that which it has already reached, and of whose necessitous state there can be no doubt? Without detriment to the work it is doing, might not a little also be done for a Heriot ragged school?

— asked the *Courant*.

The area bounded by the High Street, Cowgate, St Mary's Wynd and Niddry Street was the most densely populated district of the town. The closes were narrow, confined, dirty and very high; it was also the centre for crime and vice. The most common addresses to appear in the police records were Hyndford's Close, Blackfriars' Wynd and South Foulis' Close. Here the worst of Edinburgh's criminal fraternity lived next to many respectable people, who, due to circumstances, had reached the lowest level.

Extreme filth was evident and the overhanging wooden house fronts in some instances filled these narrow passageways, preventing light or even fresh air from penetrating the darkness. These appendices were not part of the original design, and their removal would go some way towards improving the situation. The Council were, to a certain degree, criticised for allowing the filth to accumulate, the problem being that there were only two scavengers in the area, where it would require a dozen men to do the job satisfactorily. Regulations did exist requiring the tenants to sweep and wash the stair on a regular basis, but this could not be done —none of the residents had a brush!

Cant's Close, one of the narrowest thoroughfares in the town, was only three feet six inches wide but stood six and seven storeys high. The houses were of substantial construction, the stairs were in good condition, but very dark. Despite living on the top floor a widow, who worked as a shirt-maker, told the reporter that she required artificial light when she was working. This woman explained that she was paid $4^1/_2$d for each shirt and after deducting her overheads for thread, light and heating, her reward was two pence for an eight-hour day. In nearby Dickson's Close lived a basketmaker and a sweep who each paid an annual rent of £4. The former earned between one and two shillings (5p and 10p) a day, but complained that he had received an account for six shillings (30p) in respect of Poors' rates.

Blackfriars Wynd had at one time been a centre for the Roman Catholic ecclesiastics, with residences, chapels and other church buildings. But these uses had been abandoned. Some buildings

The plaque at the corner of Blackfriars Street and the Cowgate, which marks the site of Cardinal Beaton's Palace.

had been removed, while others were subdivided into dwellings. Among those which had survived was Cardinal Beaton's Palace at the corner of Blackfriars Wynd and the Cowgate. Sadly this structure had deteriorated significantly. The first floor of this formerly distinguished residence was occupied by a shoemaker at a rent of £12 a year. Evidence of the former church use was revealed by the presence on the wall of a framed photograph of the late Bishop Gillis. What had once been the wine cellar had been converted into houses. Halfway up the Wynd, a former chapel had been subdivided — very badly — and one of the passages had been partitioned into rooms which were let at one shilling (5p) a week. In one of these apartments lived a gardener, his wife and five children; their accommodation measured only twelve feet by five feet. There had been an outbreak of cholera in this vicinity resulting in the death of a mother and two children.

In an open space between Blackfriars Wynd and Todrick's Wynd was dumped the filth from the surrounding area. It was alleged that the rubbish was removed daily but this was questionable. The main occupation for those who could find work was hawking fish, fruit and firewood. Eating houses abounded in the area and they were renowned for their tripe suppers, 'as muckle as a man can eat' for one penny. Also on the menu was a plate of potatoes for the same price, and it could be washed down with a champagne bottle of skeechan (treacle beer) for another halfpenny.

Crime was prevalent in the vicinity, and gangs were on the streets looking for drunks who would be dragged into the nearest close and robbed — if they had anything worth stealing. The police believed that these criminals could obtain enough money by this method on a Saturday night/Sunday morning to live for the remainder of the week. Several houses had been identified as the haunts of known thieves. One Sunday evening the intrepid newspaper reporter (accompanied by two detectives and a policeman) visited two of these dens. In one he saw a number of youngsters, well known to the police as thieves, seated round a corner of a room, and silence descended as the group entered the room. Furniture consisted of two tables, a few chairs and beds of sorts. Sitting beside a fire was a young woman, aged about twenty, who was in charge of the premises. She had convictions, had spent time in jail and was installed in the house to carry the rap for any detected crimes associated with the house. Her duties included selling drink, for which she received a small percentage of the takings.

In the second house visited, the only occupant was a young woman who was reading a book. But as the visitors left the premises and walked to the end of the close in Blackfriars Wynd, the police identified the gang who used the house as their meeting place. Similar circumstances prevailed in Todrick's Wynd, Hyndford's Close and South Foulis Close. These closes and the stairs leading from them to the upper storeys were in complete darkness and entry would have been impossible (and dangerous) without the assistance of the policeman's bull's-eye light. What had been windows on the stairs were now nothing more than openings, and several deaths (accidental or suspicious) had been reported to the police.

Despite the sordid reputation of this area, children were 'oot playin'' at two o'clock on a Sunday morning. They were aged between seven and twelve and no one seemed to know, or care, who their parents were. A great deal of effort had been made by the parish minister the Revd Maxwell Nicholson, who had set up the Tron Church Industrial School. This establishment, in existence for several years, was very successful in training and finding work for girls who might otherwise have finished up on the streets. The older girls were trained in kitchen and laundry work and in the relatively short time the school had been in existence, 100 girls had been found employment. At the time of the report a further 120 were attending the school. There had been very few bad reports from employers.

The south side of the Canongate beyond St Mary's Wynd, although relatively free from vice, suffered greatly from poverty. Many families relied on soup kitchens for their food. Unfortunately this was a system which was open to abuse. Most families were grateful, but a few sacrificed their meal by selling the tickets and using the money (usually a halfpenny) to buy drink. Rents in this area ranged between sixpence ($2^{1}/_{2}$p) and one shilling-and-six-pence ($7^{1}/_{2}$p) a week. Some of the problems were, however, self-inflicted. One man earning 25 shillings a week rented a house for £9 per annum. This he considered to be beyond his means and persuaded the landlord to rent him an inferior property for £5. When, some time later, a cellar became available for a rent set at between £2–£3 a year he approached the owner with a view to using it as a house for his wife and family. The proprietor refused the request. In another instance a house-decorator, earning good wages, was living in a room measuring nine feet by three-and-a-half feet. Food for the poor was frequently tea and garvies (sprats). A mother and daughter explained that their income was derived from three sources. Part of their time was spent binding carpet shoes (slippers); for this they were paid eight pence a dozen and might complete two dozen in a week. The couple also collected 'sweepings' from warehouse floors, which consisted of paper, twine and rags. The coarse paper was taken to a shop in the New Town, and on an average week the women were likely to be paid nine pence.

Envelopes and notepaper were sold for one halfpenny a pound. Twine was purchased by the 'stick' boys at a rate of one penny a handful. Cinders were also collected and anything combustible was salvaged; the rest was thrown into the street.

Whitehorse Close, Robertson's Close, Campbell's Close, Malloch's Close, Brown's Close and Tolbooth Wynd, located on the north, lower end of the Canongate, were described as a disgrace to the city. All were open and airy, yet because of the filth that had been allowed to accumulate the smell was intolerable. There were facilities to dispose of the rubbish but many of the residents were quite content to throw the waste immediately in front of their doors. If a hole was closer than the depository it was used, thereby adding to the health problem. Rat's Close, located to the rear of Campbell's Close, was nothing more than an open sewer, built up by tenants disposing of their waste by throwing it from the windows. The only difference from times gone by was the absence of the warning cry of 'gardez-loo'; as the scavengers frequently found to their cost. Window sills were inches thick with rubbish which had gathered over a period of years. The investigators reported that 'we have seen something of the worst parts of London and of the large provincial towns of England, as well as the back slums of Dublin and Belfast, but we do not remember ever seeing anything so horribly dirty as these closes'. Lack of sufficient cleaning staff was frequently mentioned as a cause of the accumulation of so much filth, and one scavenger explained that he was expected to keep nine long closes free from rubbish — an impossible task.

It was revealed that only £8:10/- had been paid the previous year to wash the closes. Surely it was possible to wash these passageways once a month and not annually as was the case at the time of the investigations. Householders were not blameless for the situation by disposing of their refuse outwith the regulation time of morning and evening. But was it reasonable to expect these people to keep smelly rubbish in their houses?

A great deal of criticism was levelled at proprietors for their greed. The sub-division of property could be achieved at very little cost, but this could result in rental increases of 100 per cent. It was imperative, insisted the newspaper, that the council take action in terms of the Provisional Order, to have many of these subdivisions removed. The quality of the work came in for criticism and demonstrated adequately when one of the 'walls' was moved by the touch of a finger. Profiteering was rife; a room and closet was rented for £5:10s but by installing a partition the owner was able to demand £4:5s for the bigger room and £3 in respect of the dark, sloping closet.

The poorest families in this area were living in High School Wynd and the breadwinner was usually employed in labouring jobs. Incomes varied between half-a-crown (12^1/$_2$p) and fifteen shillings (75p) a week, depending on the availability of work. At the foot of High School Wynd lived a widow with seven children, one born five months after the death of her husband. The accommodation consisted of a sunken cellar, but she was an independent woman who managed to live without the need of public support 'except during a few weeks when the children had fever and measles'. This courageous woman travelled regularly to Leith where she purchased casks for one shilling (5p) each. These she broke up and made into bundles of sticks which she sold to the shopkeepers as firewood. The proud woman did not approve of sending her children round the doors to sell the wood, although by so doing her income would have been greater. The oldest of the family was a boy aged twelve who had a regular income of 2/6 (12^1/$_2$p) earned from 'going messages' and he also assisted his mother in preparing the firewood. Life was hard for the family; the children were sparsely clothed and bare-footed.

Bull's Close in the Cowgate had seen better days but in the mid-19th century it was notorious for its filth. The once fine wooden-fronted dwellings were in reality beyond habitation. Yet in the midst of the squalor there was a gem. Not far distant lived Mary Pyper, over 70 years of age, slightly-built and blind. But Mary had achieved something in life, for she was successful poetess. Her father had enlisted in the army, was believed to have been posted abroad, and from that time all contact was lost. Mary Pyper obtained a limited education, thanks to the efforts of the church elder, and she had a particular interest in poetry. She had a knowledge of Shakespeare, Milton and Thomson. Burns, she described as being 'often rather coarse'. This remarkable woman was a lady of principle, and after the death of her mother and working hard to achieve a reasonable standard of life, Mary struggled to pay off a debt for which she was not legally responsible. On being given this advice, Mary replied: 'There's a law within us that tells us what's richt an' what's wrong; I got a share o' the benefit, an' I'm entitled to pay it'.

Mary Pyper's mother had been confined to bed for six years and the daughter had the responsibility of looking after her and earning enough to provide for two. During the time of her mother's illness, Mary turned to writing poetry. Attempts to obtain subscribers were usually met with polite refusals which, in a moment of frustration, prompted her to write:

> I asked a lady to subscribe;
> She answered — She would see.
> But oh! I find she still is blind
> Alas! for her and me.

In time, however, Mary Pyper's persistence brought success, with Elliot of Princes Street accepting responsibility for publishing while Constable undertook the printing. Both gentlemen gave all profits to the poetess. Dean Ramsay, in an introduction to the volume, wrote that the poems are 'of no common order of excellence, both in diction and sentiments'.

Mary's writing was recognised far beyond Edinburgh and a number of her poems appeared in an English hymn book entitled *Lays of the Pious Minstrels.*

> An Epitaph — A Life
>
> I came at morn — 'twas Spring, I smiled;
> The fields with green were clad;
> I walked abroad at Noon — and, lo!
> 'Twas Summer — I was glad.
> I sate me down — 'twas Autumn eve,
> And I with sadness wept;
> I laid me down at Night, and then
> Twas Winter —and I slept!

Mary Pyper's volume of poems ran to at least three editions. Nearby lived another woman who occupied a 'room' which in fact consisted of a small part of a partitioned lobby. Her accommodation measured eight feet by four-and-a-half feet. Her bed consisted of straw and rags which lay in a corner and the floor was cluttered with jars and pieces of crockery. This woman's only companion was a cat which entered and left the 'flat' by way of a hole in the roof. Yet despite her frugal way of life this woman must have had a reasonable education, for she enjoyed a small income working as an 'amanuensis'; in other words she wrote letters on behalf of others who were incapable of performing such a simple task. As evidence of her occupation, pens and ink bottles stood on a shelf. This woman's background was a mystery, but there was a suspicion that at one time she had enjoyed a much higher standard of living.

Despite the appalling conditions in which residents of the Old Town were forced to live, there was evidence of a great deal of creative ability. James Annan was a shoemaker who lived in the vicinity of Blair Street. When business was slack, and that was frequently, Annan resorted to writing poetry. He described himself as one of 'nature's poets' and humorously complained that poets before him had used up the primroses and daisies in their works, but he was not dismayed for there were nettles and dockens! A verse from one of the shoemaker's poems read;

> The mountain steep where wild flowers blaw,
> And purple heather bloom;
> A singing linn does gently fa'
> 'Mang banks o' yellow broom.

Annan spent several years on the stage before deserting the boards. Did he regret that decision? He was philosophical in his response — those he had known in that profession had been dead for twenty years!

A Stevenlaw's Close had existed for centuries, and at one time had been the abode of Edinburgh's wealthy merchants, but by the mid-1800s things had changed considerably. Here could be found some of the worst living conditions in the town — and the rents were high. Poverty abounded, work was unobtainable, and consequently food was scarce. When the investigators called at one flat, they found a family consisting of mother, father and five children; they were having breakfast — at two in the afternoon. The family had to wait until the mother returned with a little money earned by selling sprats. None of the family had attended school, the bed was covered by a single covering, and this was the only bed in the house. Clothing was sparse and furniture non-existent.

Public assistance was difficult to obtain because of bureaucracy. Relief could be refused by the Parochial Board because a wife refused to go to the area where her husband was born or declined to be admitted to the poorhouse.

Moving away from the town centre, the area of Greenside was recognised as being undesirable. Many of the houses were described as being 'dark, damp and uncomfortable, particularly those which are sunk three or four storeys below the level of the main thoroughfare.' The drainage was in a very poor state and back lanes and courts were 'abominably dirty'. Yet many of these abodes were occupied by residents who, by the standards of the time, were relatively well-off, earning £2 a week. They were, however, living in atrocious conditions, paying rent of between £2 and £3 a year – in many cases to satisfy their craving for drink.

Many meaningful efforts were launched to help the poor and destitute, mainly through churches, small organisations and individuals, but these well-intended projects were uncoordinated and incapable of dealing with the vast problem. The poor and homeless were not ignored by the authorities and the House of Refuge in the Canongate and the Night Asylum in the High Street, catered for the less fortunate members of society. The 'Refuge' was maintained in a clean and tidy condition although the sleeping apartments were overcrowded. Many of the residents were elderly. Any man seeking night accommodation was required to arrive no later that 8 p.m., given a roll for supper, and taken to a room which had a wooden sleeping bench round the walls. No covering, such as blankets, was provided, and a stove was the only means of heating. The residents were expected to leave without the benefit of breakfast. Women and children were provided with porridge and milk before being turned out at 7 a.m.

In theory only strangers were admitted to the Night Asylum, which had facilities for 40 men and 40 women. The password for men was 'in search of work'; women were 'in search of husband'! Supper and breakfast were provided and each resident received a blanket. Every effort was made by the Superintendent to obtain work for these unfortunate people, and many successes were achieved. One disadvantage of closing the doors of these centres at an early hour was that someone arriving in the town, destitute, could be in the position of having no shelter for the night, although places were available, and such an individual would be forced to sleep 'rough'. Frequently space was available in the police station, but regulations prohibited the use of these premises for any one other than a prisoner.

A law-abiding citizen who spent the night at the 'Refuge' would be given a bread roll on arrival, and no other food. A prisoner held at the police station was provided with a roll and pint of milk for both supper and breakfast.

Dr Henry Littlejohn, Edinburgh's first Medical Officer, was appointed in 1862, and three years later he published his important report on the sanitary conditions of Edinburgh. Littlejohn's findings contained four fundamental conclusions. He recommended that: (1) Paving and drainage of the closes must be brought up to a satisfactory level; (2) Housing for the poor must be improved by the introduction of water and gas, the cleaning of common stairs and repairs being carried out; (3) The reduction of over-crowding by limiting the number of residents in each apartment, reducing the height of tenements and removing accommodation that was beyond repair; and (4) widening areas such as the Cowgate and St Mary's Wynd and the formation of streets which should pass at right angles to the long closes which would make cleansing easier.

William Chambers, the well-known publisher, was elected Lord Provost on 10 November 1865. He was acutely aware of the conditions which prevailed in the poor areas of the town and within a month he spoke at a Council meeting regarding sanitary improvements. There had been outbreaks of fever, and Littlejohn had, as a matter of urgency, recommended that all the closes should be flushed with water purified by the use of chloride of lime. The Lord Provost told the meeting that this action could only be considered to be a temporary expedient and that more stringent measures were required.

He said that in order to tackle this major problem it would be necessary to obtain: (1) A Provisional Order in respect of drainage and general sanitary improvements, and (2) an Act to carry out extensive structural alterations throughout the town. Lord Provost Chambers told his fellow councillors:

> Almost every day since I was elected Lord Provost I have perambulated the closes in the old town. I have scrutinised every one of them on the north side of the High Street from the North Bridge to New Street; and on the south side from the Old Fishmarket Close to St John Street. Besides going up and down these closes, looking into every accessible hole and corner and sometimes ascending stairs to

see the conditions of dwellings, I have gone to the tops of the taller buildings in order to get a good bird's-eye view of the whole concern. In these vastly interesting excursions I have been accompanied by the City Architect with his maps, and in various cases have had the satisfaction to go in company with the Dean of Guild and other members of the sub-committee charged with the duty of making these investigations. So far as I have gone I can fully bear out the published opinions of Dr Littlejohn as to be the absolute necessity for opening up the closes. The great question is, how are the closes to be opened up; for that lies at the basis of all sanitary reform.

His proposals were radical and included the removal of large sections of old closes to make way for more functional roadways.

The Edinburgh City Improvement Act received Royal assent on 31 May 1867 and affected areas which included what is now St Mary's Street, Jeffrey Street and Chambers Street. Considerably more than £500,000 was expended on the scheme and this was reflected in the rates' bills.

In putting forward his proposals the Lord Provost admitted that it would result in an increase in the rate burden, perhaps a few pence in the pound for six or seven years. Chambers said:

I fear that many of the inhabitants consider that they are taxed enough already, but be that as it may, there is here a great, I should almost say a blessed object to be gained and we shall render the whole city more healthy, improve its appearance and doubtless extend its trade and resources.

Among the streets affected were Market Street, Cranston Street, Jeffrey Street, Blackfriars Street, St Mary's Street, Guthrie Street, Lady Lawson Street, Marshall Street and Howden Street. Chambers, one of Edinburgh's more enterprising Lord Provosts, is remembered by Chambers Street, which also formed part of the improvement scheme, and on 5 March 1891 a statue was unveiled there in acknowledgement of his work. Further evidence of Old Town improvements of more recent times can be seen on that stretch of streets between the castle and Holyrood.

The series of articles which appeared in the *Courant* during the period 1866-67 resulted in contributions in the region of £100 being sent to the paper spontaneously for distribution among needy families. It had never been intended to establish an official fund and in time all contributions had been allocated.

The Courant *campaign for better housing was successful, as this plaque at the top of St Mary's Street proves.*

Then in 1883 Mr Harris contacted the *Courant* regarding the plight of children in the Old Town. This gentleman ran the West Port Refreshment Room and was well aware of the suffering of many of the children in the vicinity. On 13 March the paper carried a story exposing the situation. Next day two letters appeared in the *Courant* urging that immediate action be taken to alleviate the problem, and two days later a letter was received from 'A Friend' in Glasgow, enclosing twelve postage stamps as a contribution to a fund 'for the poor in the West Port'. And so, like the phoenix of mythology, The *Courant* Fund for Poor Children rose from the ashes.

In under three months a sum of £142:7:11$^{1}/_{2}$ had been subscribed to provide food for hungry children. As the newspaper pointed out, one of the characteristics of the fund was the interest that had been shown by children. Donations had come from schools, among them The Grange Academy and Institution, and the Liberton Niddrie Public School. The Children's Church connected with the Free Church at Stockbridge had also made a donation. One small girl had been responsible for two collections totalling £3:5/-, the money having been obtained from about fifty of her friends, with sums varying from between three pence to one shilling. The money had come from savings over several weeks.

One father wrote to the *Courant:*

> I am deputed by my little boys to send the enclosed 12s 6d which has been collected for the Destitute Children's Fund. The subscription began by the younger child (five years old) bringing a shilling from his box, and saying he wanted to give it for the poor children.

Another feature of the fund was that donations did not come entirely from wealthy families, and in several cases money had been sent from members of the staff in the 'big houses'. Within three months more than 500 donations had been received. As an example of what had been achieved, in one week 90 children had been provided with breakfast or dinner daily, in one of eight refreshment establishments which had agreed to participate in the scheme. But there was a problem — lack of financial resources — and harsh decisions had to be made, even within families.

Only three months after the fund had been launched, the following balance sheet was published:

Total subscriptions as acknowledged in *Courant* up to and including 11th. June	£142:7:11^{1}/$_{2}$
Bank interest received	2:3
	£142:10:2^{1}/$_{2}$
19,618 meals at 1^{1}/$_{2}$d	122:12:3
786 meals at 2d.	6:11:0
Expended on special cases	7:10:6^{1}/$_{2}$
Handed over to Miss Flora C. Stevenson for poor children	1:13:6
	138:7:3^{1}/$_{2}$
Balance in hand at 11 June	4:2:11

Edinburgh, 22d. June, 1883. — The preceding statement has been examined by us and found correct.

(Signed) Lindsay, Jamieson, & Haldane.

The significant points revealed in this account were that no charges had been made for administration and the meal tickets, several thousands had been printed, were supplied by the *Courant*.

As a further illustration of the efficient way in which the fund was managed, the refreshment room keepers were reimbursed weekly and cash was not left in bank accounts but spent on the use for which it had been intended. More than a century later the *Courant* Fund for Needy Children is still in existence.

– 13 –
SAUGHTON PRISON, AND THE MEN WHO WALKED TO THE GALLOWS

When the decision was taken that the Calton Jail had out-lived its usefulness, the authorities chose a site at Saughton, on the west side of the town, on which to build a replacement penal establishment.

The land had been purchased in 1913, and the prison was first used in 1919, but it was not until 1925 that the last of the prisoners were transferred from the Calton.

No doubt this establishment was fitted with the most sophisticated equipment then available, but the security could be breached...and it was! One prisoner walked out 42 days after he had been sent-down. Needless to say this incident caused considerable embarrassment to the prison authorities.

The escapee was Cedric Norval, who had been sentenced to 18 months' imprisonment on 16 February 1925, at the High Court in Edinburgh, for breaking into a house in Cluny Gardens in the city. It was about mid-day on Saturday 29 March when Norval, who was a member of a prison working party, gave the warders the slip.

The alarm was raised and the police were confident that Norval would be picked up quickly. Why? Because the prisoner was dressed in the distinctive uniform of blue and red striped jacket and corduroy trousers. But when Norval was arrested in Arthur Street at 7 p.m. — seven hours after his escape — he was wearing a tweed jacket and vest, overalls and a cap!

One newspaper reported: 'How he obtained these and where he had effected the change is a mystery'.

No doubt this incident would have been the subject of further police investigation and hopefully a report was submitted to the Procurator Fiscal!

When Saughton Prison was built, the development included a specially constructed cell for condemned prisoners. Adjacent was the iron-beamed scaffold which was the first permanent structure of its kind in Scotland.

The clock still stands above the entrance to Saughton Prison. On execution days vigils were held and tension rose as 8 a.m. approached.

This was an area of the prison which everyone hoped would never be required, but on 23 July 1928, that cell received its first occupants — one of four men who were to hang at Saughton for murder.

Allan Wales

Why should a clock that has stood silent and apparently broken for several years suddenly restart? In 1928 such an incident reportedly happened in a Leith house — and the following day the mother of Allan Wales, who was under sentence of death for the murder of his young, slightly-built, wife, was informed that the Secretary of State had found no evidence to justify the reprieve of her condemned son.

Mrs Wales said that she and her daughter had been sitting in the house in Seafield Avenue, when the alarm went off. It stopped only after her daughter moved the hands on the timepiece. The distraught woman was convinced that this was a warning of the news that was to follow.

On 23 July 1928, Allan Wales appeared before Lord Anderson and a jury at the High Court, Edinburgh. He was charged that, in the basement area of a house in Pirniefield Place he assaulted Isabella Wales, his wife, cut her throat with a knife or other sharp instrument, and murdered her, and further that he evinced malice and ill-will against her by repeatedly threatening, beating and assaulting her.

The trial had attracted considerable interest and long before the court opened, a long queue had formed in Parliament Square in the hope of gaining admission.

The accused was 22-years-old, sturdily built with fair hair. He had worked as a miner with the Niddrie and Benhar Coal Company but at the time of the alleged offence he was unemployed.

Mrs Hain, mother of the deceased, told the court that her daughter Isabella had married the accused on 2 December 1926, and witness admitted that she did not approve of the marriage. The couple had lived in a single room, first in Bonnington Road, and later at Thorntree Street. Mrs Hain said that Wales had frequently assaulted Isabella. On 24 October 1927, their son had been born at the Edinburgh Maternity Hospital.

Continuing her evidence, Mrs Hain said that on Saturday 2 June 1928, she and her daughter had met the accused in the Kirkgate, Leith, and he had asked his wife for sixpence. He then accused Mrs Hain of having 'mis-called' him. His outburst had caused a crowd to gather which upset her daughter, who burst into tears.

Isabella spent the weekend with relatives in St Anthony Street and, on the Monday afternoon she had asked her cousin to take the baby and wedding ring to her mother-in-law's house.

'Did your daughter tell you why?' — 'She said that she was not going back to him again. She was going to look for work in service'.

On Tuesday, 5 June, Isabella and her cousin Jessie Berry arrived in Pirniefield Place about 11 a.m. where they had met Wales. He had again asked his wife to go back with him but she had declined. Later Wales had gone to the house at Pirniefield Place in an attempt to persuade Isabella to change her mind, but she refused. He then said that his mother wanted to see her and Isabella had told him that she could call at Pirniefield Place.

The accused came back with his mother, who lived in Seafield Avenue, but they were unable to convince Isabella that she should give the marriage another chance and that she should return to the matrimonial home in Orchardfield Lane.

Asked to explain what happened next, Mrs Hain said that she was peeling potatoes at the sink and did not see Wales coming downstairs. He opened the door and came in, then gripped Isabella by the shoulder. He had a knife. He dragged her into the outside area and threw her to the ground. Witness fled upstairs in an attempt to obtain assistance, but when she returned her daughter was dead.

Andrew Hain, a stone-mason and father of the dead woman, admitted to telling his wife not to interfere in the marriage. 'Why did you tell her that?' — 'He was married to her and should have kept her.'

Jessie Berry, cousin of the deceased, told the court that Isa had asked her to take the baby to her husband at Seafield Avenue. He was not there, but she left the child with the grandmother, explaining that Isa was going into service at Newington. Witness went on to say that on the Tuesday, she and Isa had taken a tram to the corner of Pirniefield Place, where they had met Wales. Isa and Wales had spoken briefly and privately before parting. Regarding the later return of Wales to the house in Pirniefield Place, Jessie said that when the accused came into the kitchen she ran out because she was afraid of him. He had a fierce look on his face and she thought that he was going to do something. Witness was followed from the house by her aunt (Mrs Hain) and Jessie shouted for help. A man accompanied her back to the house. Five to ten minutes later the accused left, his hands and clothes covered in blood.

William King, 88 Henderson Street, said that he was on Leith Links, heard screaming, and ran over. He then went to the scene of the tragedy. The victim was receiving attention, so he followed the accused to Seafield Avenue. Mr King asked the accused what he had done and Wales allegedly replied: 'She deserved it. I will not beat about the bush', adding 'There are some people who can't mind their own business'. Wales then took a ring from his pocket and said: 'She sent me my ring back and left the kiddie for two nights'.

After their wedding (which Mrs Hain, mother of the deceased, had refused to attend) Allan and Isabella Wales set up home in a single room at 87 Bonnington Road. Their landlord admitted that the couple were not on good terms. Uncle of the deceased, John Berry, who lived at 1 St Anthony Street, told the court that because of her fear for the accused, he had advised his niece always to keep to crowded thoroughfares.

Detective Sergeant Alexander Drummond said in evidence that in response to a telephone message he went to a house in Pirniefield Place where he found the body of a young woman. Drummond then went to Seafield Avenue where the accused was pointed out to him. Wales was speaking with his sister and his hands and clothes were covered in blood. Wales was told that he was being arrested in connection with the death of his wife and to say nothing about the matter. He replied: 'I am the man'. The accused was taken to a police station, and when he was being searched he allegedly said: 'I have something for you'. Wales then produced a blood-stained cobbler's knife from inside a jacket pocket. 'He was perfectly calm and cool' the policeman told the court. On being charged, Wales replied: 'That's right'.

Dr Arthur Murray Wood said that at the time of the tragedy he was in Pirniefield Place visiting a patient. At the request of a policeman he had gone to the scene of the crime where he examined the body of a young woman and confirmed death.

Police Surgeon Douglas Kerr said that when he saw the accused he was perfectly rational but perhaps a little backward.

William Edington, an employee of an organisation connected with child welfare, told how Wales, whom he had never seen before, called at his office on 4 June (the day before the murder) and explained that his wife and child had left him and asked for assistance in persuading them to come home. Wales returned to the office next day to say that his wife had sent the child and wedding ring to his mother's address. 'Will you be seeing her today?' he had asked. Mr Edington told Wales that he would do his best. Witness added that the accused was sensible and clear in his manner.

The trial continued late into the day, and Wales was found guilty by a majority of 14 to one; but the jury added a strong recommendation for mercy on account of the convicted man's youth. Lord Anderson sentenced Wales to death, the execution to be carried out on 13 August 1928. A subsequent appeal was dismissed.

As befitting the sombre occasion the execution day dawned

with a steady drizzle falling over the city, but this did not deter a group of approximately 300 people gathering outside the prison. Those present, however, were prevented by the police from gaining access to the drive leading to the prison doors. The windows of nearby houses were used as vantage points, but what could they expect to see? The prison clock finally showed 8 a.m. and simultaneously the horn from neighbouring works sounded as if bidding a last farewell. Immediately the formal notice, signed by the Governor, Brigadier R.M. Dudgeon, and other officials, had been displayed, there was a stampede to read it and the police were forced to intervene.

But there was one final twist to this tragic affair. A well-meaning Leith businessman announced that a committee would be set-up to raise funds to pay the murdered woman's funeral expenses and erect a stone. It was also hoped that there would be enough money to bring up the nine-month-old orphan. This proposal was firmly opposed by both families. The day following the execution, Florence Hain, the murdered woman's mother, told newspapers that she 'wished no memorial stone and asks for no charity'.

The Wales family revealed that Allan Wales had 'signed a paper' for an insurance society to pay the funeral expenses in respect of Isabella Wales. The balance of the money was to be given to Mr and Mrs Wales senior, on behalf of their grandson. 'No public fund is therefore required for funeral expenses', explained Mrs Wales.

She added that they would not accept any public subscription towards the upkeep of their grandson; the family were quite willing and able to support him themselves.

Tragedy may have divided the two families, but they were certainly united in grief, pride and independence.

Robert Dobie Smith

On Saturday, 15 September 1951, Robert Dobie Smith, a Dumfries electrician, was hanged at Saughton Jail for the murder of police sergeant William Gibson on 22 May. The convicted man was later buried within the confines of the prison. This was the second hanging to take place at Edinburgh's 'new' penal establishment; the first had been carried out 23 years previously.

There were about 20 people, three of them women, outside the prison as the appointed time for execution approached. At 8.01 a.m., the statutory notice certifying that the sentence had been carried out, was posted on the outside of the building. Signatories to this document included the Revd C. McArthur Chalmers, the prison chaplain and, incidentally, minister at Carrick Knowe Church.

For some inexplicable reason, members of the public were prevented from reading the notice until forty-five minutes after it had been displayed, and several, tired of waiting, left after half-an-hour. Eventually the police relented and allowed those remaining to go forward in groups of six to examine the notice and satisfy their morbid curiosity.

It was 2.50 a.m. on 22 May 1951, when the telephone rang in Dumfries police station. The call was taken by Constable James Little, and the message was to the effect that there was a madman in Holm Avenue. In the background the policeman could hear the sound of whimpering.

He immediately alerted all beat-men, asking anyone who was in the vicinity to investigate. Sergeant William Gibson immediately returned to the station to co-ordinate plans. A later message confirmed that the suspect was Robert Dobie Smith and that he was in possession of a shot-gun.

Shortly after 4 a.m. it was reported that the wanted man had been seen in Irish Street, and sergeant Gibson, together with constables Hope and Campbell set off in a patrol car to investigate. As the vehicle turned into Bank Street, the policemen spotted a man standing erect with his back to the wall, and hiding his hands.

As constable Campbell was later to tell the High Court in Dumfries, sergeant Gibson remarked that he thought he was the man they were seeking. He stopped the car and asked the suspect what he was doing. Without warning Smith produced a gun and fired, hitting the sergeant and constable Hope who were in the front seats.

Constable Campbell, who was sitting immediately behind the sergeant, jumped out of the vehicle and overpowered the man before he could. reload the gun. Told by Campbell that he had shot sergeant Gibson, he allegedly replied: 'It's a pity it wasn't that — Duncan'. This outburst was to be explained later in court.

Despite his serious injuries, constable Hope struggled to the County Hotel, where he received assistance from the night staff. At 4.20 a.m. constable Campbell returned to the police station with the suspect, accompanied by a member of the County Hotel staff who was carrying a knife and shotgun.

Meanwhile several people had gathered at the scene and an employee of a firm of wholesale newsagents drove Gibson and Hope to the Infirmary. The sergeant was dead on arrival; constable Hope had serious injuries to both arms.

The sergeant left a widow, an 18-year-old son and a 10-year-old daughter. The son was due to sail from Tilbury that day as an apprentice deck officer. After a frantic search, the port officials found the lad as he walked through the dock area. The sergeant was 44 years of age with twenty-years' service. Sergeant Gibson's brother was a police officer at Kirkpatrick-Durham. Constable Hope was 26-years-old, married, with a young child. The two men were near-neighbours in the police houses.

Later in the day, Robert Dobie Smith appeared at Dumfries Burgh Court, charged with murder and attempted murder. It was revealed that the accused was a 31-one-year-old electrician.

The trial opened at the High Court, Dumfries, on 24 July 1951, Lord Mackay presiding. It was the first murder trial in that court for 18 years.

Smith faced three charges: (1) stealing 25 cartridges from his father's house; (2) in Bank Street, Dumfries, near the junction with High Street, shooting William Gibson, sergeant of the Dumfries and Galloway Constabulary with a shot gun in the head; and (3) shooting constable Andrew Hope in both arms. Constable James Little told the court of the telephone call and the deployment of men in an attempt to arrest the accused.

Andrew Smith, brother of the accused, said that he had gone to bed about 11 p.m. At approximately 1 a.m. his brother came into the room. The accused had a shotgun and he told witness to get up. I have something for you to do, he told his brother. Andrew Smith was then told to go to the kitchen where his brother produced the shank of a hammer from his pocket. Robert was pointing a gun at him. The accused then told his brother to go into the living room and to sit at the table.

Robert had a school jotter and told his brother to write to his instruction. He dictated: 'To Andy — all the best in the world. I hope that you will live till you are sixty and that by the time you are sixty you have stopped snoring. If you come over to this side of the table I will hit you between the eyes with this hammer.'

Dictation continued for about two hours and included: 'When I get out of this door tonight I will shoot the first policeman I see.

The right hammer is faulty but the barrel is clean'. His ramblings continued: 'I Robert Smith know how to use weapons because I had six years of killing men'. The accused had spent six years in the navy. His dictation went on: 'There was one girl. She was nineteen. She was too young. If I had married her I would have made an honest and useful citizen, but alas, I am thirty and no further use to the world'.

When the dictation was eventually finished, Andrew was told to dress and the brothers left the house. They went to a telephone box and Andrew was instructed to phone the police with the message that there was a madman in Holm Avenue. That done the younger man was told to go home.

James Kenneth MacDonald said that Smith had burst into his house in Irish Street at about 3.30 a.m. He had a shotgun and was very upset, apparently at the death of one of MacDonald's young relatives. Smith had allegedly said to MacDonald: 'They're after me. I got one and I'll get another'. Next he mumbled something about having started something and he would have to finish it.

The accused then asked for a pencil and paper. But as MacDonald moved to get them, he was ordered back to bed and to keep his hands under the bed clothes. Eventually Smith produced paper and instructed Macdonald to write: 'I wrote this under duress. I Robert Smith killed a man tonight. I held up K. MacDonald and his wife and forced then to write this'. Smith added his signature and immediately afterwards wrote: 'Dear Ken and Nan — you have been expecting this for some time. You are two of the finest people I know'.

The accused then left the house but returned a few minutes later. He told the occupants that 'they are all around me so don't make any wrong moves'. He had a hammer and breadknife in his possession.

Asked if he had any reason to believe that Smith had any animosity towards the police, Macdonald said that he had been taken to the police station regarding an incident but had been released.

Mrs Annie MacDonald told the court that she had a 19-year-old sister, Joan Gillespie, who had been engaged to Smith, but it had been broken off. He took it hard; it prayed on his mind, she said.

Constable R.J. Richardson explained that on 26 March, with sergeant Andrew Dunn, he had taken Smith to the police station with regard to loitering in suspicious circumstances. He was later released.

Advocate Depute H.R. Leslie KC, in moving sentence, said that he wished to restrict his motion to the charge of murder. In his closing speech he told the court that sergeant Gibson, inoffensive and defenceless, had been shot by Smith at a range of two feet and PC Hope's arms were seriously injured by a second shot. On the special defence that Smith was insane at the time and was not responsible for his actions, he said that it must be approached with caution.

At the end of the four day trial the Judge, Lord Mackay, in summing up, told the jury of ten women and five men that a man had been killed by a shotgun and another had been shot at to kill. It had been proved that Smith discharged the gun and the only question was one of responsibility.

The jury were out for 32 minutes before returning unanimous verdicts of murder and wounding. The charge of theft had been abandoned. The sentence was that Smith would be executed at Saughton Prison on 17 August 1951, between 8 and 10 a.m.

On 28 August the Criminal Appeal Court unanimously dismissed Smith's appeal, and the new date for execution was fixed for 15 September.

Three days before the sentence was due to be carried out, it was confirmed that the Secretary of State for Scotland, after careful consideration of the case, had been unable to find sufficient grounds to advise His Majesty to interfere with the due course of the law.

John Lynch

Greenside Row, in the 1950's had some of the poorest housing in Edinburgh. Lying in the valley between Leith Street/Walk and the Calton Hill, it stretched for approximately 300 yards and consisted of tenements with cul-de-sac, closes and alleys running off it. The site, today, is unrecognisable, with major redevelopment taking place.

This was also the scene of one of the most horrific crimes — a double child murder — ever perpetrated in the town.

The time was approaching 5 p.m. on 11 December 1953, when the police were informed that two small girls, Margaret Johnston, aged three, and four-and-a-half-year-old Lesley Sinclair were missing. They had been last seen two hours previously. Margaret lived at 9 Queen's Place and Lesley's address was 5 Marshall's Court, Greenside Row.

Neighbours joined the police in searching the congested closes and passageways which abounded in the area. Torches were used in the hunt, which extended to the bushes on the slopes of the Calton Hill. One man thought that he heard the cries of a child and climbed over a fence, but found nothing. Ironically it was directly opposite 5 Marshall's Court where the bodies of the children were found about 11 p.m.

The discovery of the dead girls shocked the neighbourhood and many, who had been in bed, rose and dressed. They stood in groups, many of them extremely distressed. In the course of what little conversation took place, it was revealed that several residents had attempted to gain access to the communal lavatory where the bodies had been found, but the door always seemed to be locked.

Police reinforcements were soon on the scene and their cars could be seen parked in the dimly gas-lit court. Policemen were on duty at the entrance to 5 Marshall's Court while others guarded the entrance to the lavatory. By a curious twist of fate, Jean Sinclair, mother of one of the dead girls had twice passed that door.

Quietly and efficiently the routine procedure of taking statements was underway, and at an early stage a bizarre incident took place. Was it conscience, tension—or guilt that caused 45-year-old John Lynch to lunge forward and launch into a loud, almost hysterical, outburst? Lynch was a labourer who lived in a flat at the address where the bodies had been found. 'Take my name; I'll tell you how it was done', he reportedly shouted.

Lynch was not at this stage a suspect and he was quietly taken back to his flat; but no doubt his actions had been noted by the police; and in the early hours of the following morning Lynch was arrested and charged with murder. He appeared at the Burgh Court and was remitted to the Sheriff.

Mr and Mrs David Curran, mother and stepfather of Margaret Johnston, told newspaper reporters that Mrs Curran had been in her mother-in-law's house at 5 Marshall's Court when Margaret came in and asked for a 'piece'. As she left, the youngster had been told to play on an area of open space where she could be seen. At about 3.20 p.m., when Mrs Curran's daughters Jeanette (10) and Irene (8) arrived from school, they had gone looking for

Margaret. Almost eight agonising hours were to pass before the body of Margaret and her friend Lesley Sinclair were found.

Residents in small communities are renowned for coming to assistance in times of disasters and emergencies and the people of Greenside were no exception.

The neighbours immediately set up a fund for the bereaved families and it was hoped to raise £100. When it closed a few days later, £125 had been collected. At Lady Glenorchy's Church, where the girls attended Sunday School, children gave their pocket money to buy a wreath.

On the morning of 16 December, mourners attended the funeral of Lesley Sinclair at Liberton Cemetery. Earlier, 400 people stood, heads bowed, as Lesley's pathetically small, white coffin was taken from the undertakers at Greenside Place. Later that day Margaret Johnston was laid to rest at the Eastern Cemetery. Two hundred people were present.

The trial of stockily-built, grey-haired, John Lynch opened at the High Court on 23 March, 1954. It was to last for three days.

Mrs Jean Sinclair told the court that she had reported her daughter missing about 4.45 p.m. At 5.30 p.m. she located her husband in a Leith Street pub where he had called for a drink on his way home from work. He was in the company of John Lynch.

She called her husband over, and curiously Lynch came with him. Mrs Sinclair explained the situation and in an attempt to comfort his wife, the husband told her not to worry. Lynch had allegedly retorted: 'Can't you see that Mrs Sinclair is worried'. Turning to Mrs Sinclair the accused said: 'I'll buy you a drink to pick you up'.

While Mr Sinclair went to buy a newspaper Lynch accompanied Mrs Sinclair home. On the way Lynch had told Mrs Sinclair that he had seen the two girls earlier in the afternoon. 'They all knew him', Mrs Sinclair told the court, 'They called him uncle Paddy. He was a friendly man.'

Continuing her evidence, Mrs Sinclair said that about 11 p.m. the shout had gone up that they [the children] had been found. Someone put Lesley's body into her arms. She immediately passed the dead child to her husband, then collapsed.

John Robieson, a newsvendor, took the other child, Margaret Johnston, to the home of her grandmother who lived on the same top-landing where the bodies had. been found.

Margaret McKail, whose daughter discovered the girls, said that about tea-time she had heard Lynch's voice and loud banging which could have been the lavatory door. Later that night the daughter told her mother that the lavatory door was locked. This, witness explained, happened frequently because of a defective lock. She gave her daughter a knife to pick the lock. The girl returned almost immediately to tell her mother that there was somebody lying in the toilet.

Annie Hall, who shared a flat with Lynch, said that when she left for work, a pair of her stockings were hanging in a prominent place. When she returned, one was missing. She identified a stocking in court and confirmed hearing Lynch's outburst regarding his involvement in the crime. A piece of floral cloth, taken from the neck of one girl, matched material found in the flat where the accused was living. The jury took only 55 minutes to reach their unanimous verdict of guilty, and John Lynch was sentenced to be hanged at Saughton Prison on 15 April 1954.

As Lord Thomson passed judgement he lifted the black three-cornered cap, and, holding it over his head, added the words 'which is pronounced for doom' A subsequent appeal was dismissed.

The morning of 23 April 1954, was sunless, and a cold wind was blowing outside Saughton Prison as 8 a.m. approached. A lone policeman patrolled the drive and a few spectators, newspaper reporters and photographers gathered outside the main gate. At 8.03 a.m. a man in civilian clothes emerged through a small door and pinned up the notice certifying that the due course of the law had been carried out. John Lynch, the double child murderer was dead. Later his body was buried within the confines of the prison. He was the third person to be hanged at Saughton in 26 years.

George Alexander Robertson

George Alexander Robertson must have been familiar with the location of Edinburgh's High Court, immediately behind St Giles' Cathedral. After all his future wife lived in Tron Square, a short distance away, and in his courting days he surely walked down the High Street on his way to meet her. But could Robertson ever have believed that one day he would stand in the dock of that very court, charged with the murder of his now former wife (they were divorced in 1950), their son George, and the attempted murder of daughter Jean in Tron Square on 28 February 1954?

A quiet corner in Tron Square.

As murder investigations go, it was an uncomplicated case and Robertson was arrested within minutes. But it shocked the close-knit community, not only because they knew everyone involved, but also on account of the ferocious, frenzied nature of the attacks.

At the time of the crime, newspaper reporters working on the story could find no-one living in this small enclave just off the High Street who was prepared to speak. Approximately forty windows overlooked the square, but apparently no resident saw or heard anything. One neighbour, who lived immediately opposite to where the murder had taken place, reluctantly admitted that about 2 a.m. he was awakened by screaming and smashing glass but chose to ignore it.

The dead mother had been one of the organisers for the Tron Square Coronation celebrations, and above her flat was the now faded picture of the Queen. Sadly, the mother (and grandmother) of the two victims also lived in Tron Square but several hours were to pass before the 78-year-old woman was told of the tragedy. Meanwhile police photographers were busy at the scene, while groups of children played close by. Hanging from a window were two knotted blood-stained bed spreads — evidence of a pathetic attempt to escape the carnage.

On 1 March 1954, 40-year-old George Alexander Robertson appeared before the Burgh Court and was remitted to the Sheriff without plea. At the Sheriff Court, Robertson indicated that he wanted to plead guilty, but he was not allowed to do so; this point was to be raised again at his trial.

The two-day trial opened at the High Court on 1 June 1954 before Lord Thomson, the Lord Justice Clerk. Robertson faced three charges; (1) the murder of his 39-year-old former wife Elizabeth; (2) the murder of his 18-year-old son, George, a coal porter who was awaiting his call-up for National Service, and (3) the attempted murder of his 16-year-old daughter, Jean, who worked for a firm of paper manufacturers. The trial had caught the imagination of the public, and hours before the case was due to start, a queue had formed in Parliament Square.

Jean Robertson, the first witness, told the court that her parents had divorced. At the time of her death her mother was Mrs McGarry but her father had been living with them in Tron Square. Following a dispute with her mother, Robertson had left and had not returned before that fateful 28 February.

'Were you afraid of him coming back?', she was asked. 'Yes', she replied.

'Did you take any steps to prevent him coming back?' 'Yes, we bolted the door. We put a poker in the window. We put a chair behind the door.'

But on the night of the murder they had forgotten to put the chair behind the door. Jean Robertson was awakened by the voice of her father telling her mother in a whisper to 'go ben the kitchen'. Witness said that she then wakened her brother and they went into the lobby.

'What did you see in the lobby?', she was asked. Shaking her head and crying, Jean described how she saw her father use a knife on George, who fell. He then turned on the witness, pushing her onto a bed and began stabbing her. Jean Robertson explained to the court that she had injuries to the left side of her stomach and her arm: 'I was screaming. I then heard the outside door being opened. My father rushed out and went downstairs. George was sitting on a chair and he asked me to get a doctor.'

Miss Robertson went on to say that she had tied two bedspreads together and hung them out of the window to climb down, but she was unable to use her left arm. Next was the sound of a window being smashed and Jean 'ran ben the kitchen and went out'. There she saw her father carrying her mother over his shoulder and putting her down beside the cooker. Her mother did not move. Robertson later returned with George and told Jean to get some hot water. Accused said that he would revive him with whisky and water.

A neighbour, Catherine Hay, said that Mrs McGarry (the deceased) had told her several times that Robertson had threatened to kill the family with a hatchet.

On the night of the murder Mrs Hay had been in bed and had heard the kitchen window being broken. George Robertson appeared in the house shouting 'Larry, Larry'. He was followed by the accused who had a knife in each hand. Her husband Lawrence had attempted to pull Robertson back but had been warned to keep out of it or he would get it too. The accused took his son away but returned soon afterwards asking for bandages. He warned the Hays that if they went for the police, they would find his former wife and himself dead.

Detective Sergeant Walter Middlemist said that at 2.37 a.m. Mr and Mrs Hay had arrived at the Central Police Office in the High Street. They were excited — almost hysterical. Accompanied by three policemen he had gone to the scene and found heavy blood-staining on the concrete footway. At one point there were naked foot prints in the blood.

The policemen then went to Mrs McGarry's door but got no response although they heard movement. They entered the flat and found the body of Mrs McGarry. Jean was in the flat and George was sitting on a chair. He had a wound in the region of the heart. The accused was lying on the floor with his head in the oven; he was unconscious and there was a strong smell of gas.

Medical evidence confirmed that Mrs McGarry had 15 wounds and George 14 — one through the heart. The jury took one hour to reach their unanimous verdict of guilty.

After Lord Thomson had passed the death sentence, Robertson asked permission to speak. In a steady voice he said 'It could have saved a lot of misery if, under the Scottish Act, Section 31, which gives a prisoner the opportunity to plead Guilty to crimes, I took advantage of this when I heard that I was charged with murder.

'I took advantage of this to forward a letter to the Department asking them to accept this plea to save any more grief to her family and my own and my mother. I think that it is only right if you can in any way help a man in my position again; he may have an opportunity to plead guilty. That is all. I beg to thank Mr Sloan (defence counsel).'

Robertson, who was of medium height with dark, wavy hair, was hanged at Saughton on 23 June 1954, the last man to take that short walk in Edinburgh's jail.

The formal notice of execution was pinned up in a glass-fronted noticeboard, a few minutes after 8 a.m. It read:

> We the undersigned, declare that the sentence of death was this day executed on George Alexander Robertson in the Prison of Edinburgh in our presence. Dated this 23rd. day of June 1954.

The document was signed by two bailies, the prison governor and Chaplain. Beneath was a certificate of death signed by the prison medical officer. As a precaution, a policeman and prison officer were on duty outside the prison, but few spectators were present.

Where is Their Final Resting Place?

Allan Wales, Robert Dobie Smith, John Lynch and George Alexander Robertson are buried in unmarked graves within the grounds of Saughton Prison; but where is the precise location? The answer to that sensitive question is known to a small number of officials and they guard this information with the utmost secrecy.

– 14 –
THE MYSTERIOUS VISITOR
TO ROSEBANK CEMETERY

On infrequent occasions during the second half of the nineteenth century, a closed horse-drawn carriage could be seen entering Rosebank Cemetery which is located at the junction of Pilrig Street and Broughton Road. The coach was driven slowly and reverently along the pathway with the loose covering being churned up by the weight of the vehicle and the horses' hooves as they dug into the surface, the animals struggling to keep the coach moving, encouraged by a considerate and sympathetic coachman.

In a few minutes they reached a point, approximately in the centre of the cemetery and halted in front of a pair of comparatively simple gravestones. A coachman dismounted, opened the carriage door and assisted a small, slightly plump woman in dark clothes to alight. This task completed, the servant turned away and joined the other members of the small party who had retired discreetly a few yards distant.

That lady stood before the two memorials, head bowed on a fine autumn day, alone with her private thoughts. It was a still, sunny day and the peace was disturbed just occasionally by the snorting of one or other of the horses or the chirping of birds as they flitted among the stones oblivious of the sombre occasion.

What went through the head of that relatively young woman will never be known; memories of a woman only three years the mourner's senior who had died so suddenly in Edinburgh. She was German by birth but the pair had worked closely sharing much enjoyment and no doubt personal secrets.

The second grave contained the remains of a man who perhaps was more fortunate, having survived seventy-two years, no mean achievement in the nineteenth century.

In due course, her contemplation's completed, the lady raised her head, a signal quickly seen by the observant coachman, to announce that the visit was finished, and he walked the few steps to the coach, opened the door and assisted the mourner into her seat, soon to be joined by the other members of the group. The coachman then joined the horseman, who had brought the relaxing animals back under his control. There was a pause lasting several seconds, then, following only the slightest sign of a final wave and bow, the vehicle was driven out of Rosebank Cemetery and headed for home. Nothing unusual in that you might think, except that lady was Queen Victoria. And the purpose of that visit by Her Majesty? She was there to pay her respects to two Royal servants whose last resting place is Rosebank.

On 13 October, 1854, Queen Victoria left Edinburgh and returned to London, leaving her dresser Ida Bonanomi who was ill. Could Victoria have realised just how seriously ill Miss Bonanomi was and that only two days later she was to die at number nine Princes Street? The Queen, who was ages with her faithful servant, was obviously deeply upset at the loss of a woman who was probably just as much a companion as a member of the staff. And so in due course Ida Bonanomi was laid to rest at Rosebank. Why Rosebank? That is a mystery, but the explanation might be that Rosebank was a relatively new cemetery, opened only eight years previously, and where, at that time, the land was a vast open green field in the middle of a town. This could not have been obtained in any of the older graveyards and so there she lies, Ida Bonanomi, a servant who had known the palaces of Britain, among the shipowners, businessmen and other folk who had been born, worked and died in Leith.

In time Victoria remembered her dresser in a permanent way by erecting a relatively simple stone over her grave with the equally simple but adequate inscription which reads:

Sacred to the memory of Miss Ida Bonanomi the faithful and highly esteemed dresser of Queen Victoria who departed this life Octr. 15th 1854 in the 37th year of her age beloved and respected by all who knew her.

This stone has been placed by Queen Victoria as a mark of her regard.

Immediately to the right there is a second memorial with the following inscription:

Sacred to the memory of Owen Couch who died at Holyrood Palace on 9th November 1872 aged 72 years. He was a faithful servant in the household of their majesties George IV William IV and Victoria for upwards of fifty years.

Also of Mary Jupp his wife who died at Musselburgh on 11th March 1875 aged 73 years.

Was it coincidence or is there a more simple explanation why two Royal servants should be buried in adjoining graves? Perhaps palace officials were aware that the land acquired in 1854 was sufficiently large to allow the burial of two families and as a mark of respect and in consideration of his long service to the throne, the lair was made available for the interment of Owen Couch and later his wife.

Fifty years is a long time to spend in one job, and in the case of Owen Couch this meant serving three monarchs. What indiscretions did he overhear, remembered but never revealed as he attended to the needs of two kings and a queen, for although he died at Holyrood, Owen Couch must have spent some of his working life at Buckingham Palace, which was bought by George III in 1762. He would have remembered George IV, debtor, his liaison with Mrs Fitzherbert and builder of the Brighton Pavilion. George died in 1830 and was followed by William IV, third son of George III. Owen Couch would have remembered William as a statesman who refused to swamp the majority in the House of Lords and which had rejected the Reform Bill in 1832. And of course Victoria. Couch must have heard many stories and rumours in the rooms and corridors of the palaces but to this faithful servant they remained just that.

The graves of the two royal servants can be found with no difficulty. From the main entrance in Pilrig Street walk straight ahead for perhaps two hundred yards, then take the tarred pathway to the right. Count the stones which face directly on to the access and the 'royal' memorials are thirteen and fourteen along the line.

Queen Victoria's visits to Rosebank cemetery were strictly private and therefore the number is unknown. On 7 August 1860, however, the Queen reviewed Army Volunteers in the Queen's Park. There were 20,000 troops present, and accompanying the Queen were Albert, Princesses Alice, Helena and Louise, and Prince Arthur.

And it has been recorded that on 17 September Victoria was seen leaving Rosebank accompanied by Lady Churchill and Lord Charles Fitzroy, 'this visit being neither the first nor the second'.

One journal was to report: 'There is something very touching as well as endearing in the feeling which prompts the Queen of Great Britain to secure an hour, whenever possible, to visit the last resting place of her humble handmaid.'

– 15 –
AN ELECTION — AND
THE RIOT ACT IS READ

Come election time, be it parliamentary or local, Edinburgh is not exactly ablaze with enthusiasm, electioneering or canvassing, and this apathy is usually reflected in the relatively low turn-out. This, the politicians will explain through a press release (faxed of course and from a PR person) that trends have altered and what with massive TV, radio and newspaper coverage (the media) the once popular hustings, meetings and 'door-knocking' no longer play a part in modern politics. In truth, there is a general apathy on the part of the electors.

How different from a parliamentary election which was held a little over one 160 years ago when, dissatisfied with the result and the method by which it had been achieved, Edinburgh citizens went on the rampage, there were ugly scenes, the Lord Provost was threatened with violence and indeed assaulted, and military detachments were called out to assist the police to maintain order. Eventually, after many hours of disruption, order was restored, but only after the Riot Act had been read. At that time, of course, the citizens of Edinburgh had no say in the decision — authority was vested in the Town Council!

The date was 3 May 1831, and for the last time the Town Council assembled to carry out this important duty. They were selecting the man who would replace William Dundas, who had been the Scottish capital's representative in Parliament for the previous 24 years. There were three candidates, Robert Adam Dundas, nephew of the retiring member, Lord Advocate Francis Jeffrey and Lord Provost William Allan, considered by most to be an outsider.

Dundas was not popular for it was believed that his uncle, then Member of Parliament, had voted against the Reform Bill, and consequently Jeffrey was the popular candidate among Edinburgh's residents.

The councillors treated their duties very seriously and the full council (33 members) turned up at the City Chambers for that historic vote. The day started with a service at St Giles' Cathedral. About 11 a.m. spectators began to assemble outside the council offices and very quickly the area was packed to capacity. The hands of the Tron clock were approaching 11.30 a.m. and a roar went up from the crowd as the popular Lord Advocate was spotted in the vicinity. His arrival was the signal for those present to voice their opinion on the suitability of the two main contenders. Dundas was believed to be in the Chambers and it was rumoured that he had enjoyed breakfast with some of the councillors.

Shortly before noon there was a rush for the few public seats which were available, when the news went round that the Council were assembling. At noon, precisely, the Lord Provost opened the meeting by stating that before dealing with the main part of the business, he had to announce that a number of petitions had been received and he instructed the Clerk to read them. They contained 17,000 signatures — all in favour of Jeffrey.

This formality completed, the Lord Provost called for nomination of candidates to represent the City of Edinburgh in the House of Commons.

The name R.A. Dundas was put forward and that was the signal for another outburst of hostility; Jeffrey's nomination on the other hand was warmly received. Lord Provost Allan's candidature was noted with indifference.

The vote was taken, and result was: Dundas 17; Jeffrey 14 and Allan 2. In a flash the news was conveyed to the highly charged crowd in the quadrangle and immediately all hell let loose.

'A rope, a rope for Dundas', 'Burke the Provost' and 'Burn the Bailies' were only a few of the threats which could be heard coming from the menacing throng, and an attempt was made by the mob to rush the Council chamber. Fortunately for those within, the attack was thwarted.

A considerable time elapsed before it was considered safe for the Lord Provost to leave the building, and it was only with difficulty that a passage was cleared through the throng. Strangely, in view of the tension which still prevailed among the crowd, Lord Provost Allan decided to walk to his home in Hillside Crescent, something he was to regret for the rest of his life! Gravely, and accompanied by a number of his friends, no doubt for moral support, and with a strong police presence, he struggled down the High Street and into the North Bridge.

The crowd were still in an angry mood and as he crossed the North Bridge, the police cordon was broken, the Lord Provost manhandled, and for a time it was feared that his life was in danger. Eventually the police regained control of the situation, but the outraged citizens pursued their quarry, throwing stones. In Leith Street, Edinburgh's first citizen was struck several times and eventually had to seek refuge in a shop. In the meantime the Sheriff had been summoned and he arrived accompanied by Captain Stewart. By now the crowd had turned their wrath on the police, and Stewart was badly injured. Finally the Riot Act was read, but to no avail.

A company of Irish Dragoons was rushed from Piershill Barracks, and under the protection of these soldiers the Lord Provost arrived home. Meanwhile, troops from the 79th Highlanders were ordered to the Assembly Rooms and others took up positions opposite the City Chambers.

Despite the vast crowd which had pursued the Lord Provost many thousands had remained in the vicinity of the Chambers awaiting the departure of Jeffrey, the defeated candidate. As he left the building the noise was deafening. He was followed by his supporters to the Mound where his coach was waiting and no sooner was he aboard, and to his utter astonishment, the horses were removed from the traces; immediately a group of men set off pulling the vehicle to Jeffrey's home in Moray Place. He thanked those concerned for the gesture and went indoors, but the assembled citizens would not disperse. Eventually Jeffrey appeared on the balcony and addressed the multitude:

> My friends. I sincerely thank you for this demonstration of your approbation; but may I recommend you to be peaceful and quiet and to confine yourselves to the cheering with which you have now greeted me. In less than another year I trust we shall come home better pleased with the result than we have done today. As you value my favour — as you esteem your own character — and the great cause in which we are all engaged — go quietly home and let it not be said by your adversaries that, in your call for liberty, you only mean riot and discord. Again let me beseech you to refrain from violence; we have our opinions and our opponents have theirs. They have given an erroneous one in my estimation; but let there be no personal violence. Let them enjoy their momentary and solitary triumph; for ours is the prevailing opinion and I have no doubt we

will succeed. I am much fatigued by the proceedings of this day and I hope you will excuse me not addressing you at farther length, but I again entreat, go all quietly to your homes.

Jeffrey's persuasive eloquence was successful and the crowd quietly dispersed.

But all was quite different in other parts of the town, however, where an explosive atmosphere prevailed. At 6 p.m. the Dragoons were called out once more and they were supported by a Naval detachment from Leith. Another three hours were to pass before any sign of peace was to return to the streets. As midnight approached, more than twelve hours since the incidents in one of Edinburgh's most explosive days had commenced, the demonstrators had tired, and gradually went home, and by the early hours of the following morning only a handful remained on the streets.

Surprisingly, relatively little damage had been done by the demonstrators. Dundas, the newly elected MP had several windows smashed at his house and a number of street lights had been subjected to the frustration of a small number of citizens.

But one man was conspicuous by his absence — R.A. Dundas, M.P. Where was the obligatory victorious candidate's speech thanking his supporters and assuring all of Edinburgh's citizens that he would do all in his power to safe-guard the interests of Edinburgh, the Capital of Scotland? So far as could be established, Dundas was still in the City Chambers where he had been since early morning — afraid to meet the citizens who had not elected him!

Surprisingly, only one rioter appeared in court, and was sentenced to nine months imprisonment. Shortly afterwards, Lord Provost Allan's term of office came to an end (he had served his two years) and John Learmonth became the city's Lord Provost.

The following year was a momentous one, with the passing of the Reform Bill, which had a considerable effect on electing the Members of Parliament. The year was 1832 and it was reported that on one Sunday countless thousands of citizens assembled on Calton Hill, eagerly awaiting the arrival of the express with the latest news. Eventually it was established that Edinburgh would have two representatives in Parliament.

There were three candidates, Francis Jeffrey and James Abercromby nominated by the Whigs (similar to the present day Liberals) and Forbes Hunter Blair (Tory).

The result proved how much the Town Council had been out of touch with the wishes of the people when, in 1831, they had elected Dundas. When the result was announced on 21 December 1832 the figures were: Jeffrey 4,036; Abercromby 3,843 and Blair 1,519. Both Reform candidates had been successful.

Following the announcement, Jeffrey told the assembled audience:

> It [the result] is the triumph, not of one man, or any set of men, but the triumph of principles, held in common among all free men of the earth. It is not the triumph of any party, however numerous or respectable in Edinburgh, but the triumph of a cause which has been rapidly advancing in every corner of the universe — and on the progress of which alone can be confirmed, the cause of liberty, independence, justice, peace, tolerance and intellectual improvement.

Abercromby said that 'The contest in which we have been engaged has now happily concluded and I do most heartily congratulate you on the triumph which we have gained.'

The two elected members were then taken in triumph, by coach, to Jeffrey's house in Moray Place.

The result was received with considerable enthusiasm by one newspaper which commented:

> Fellow Citizens — Let us congratulate one another! The day is our own. Toryism has made its last expiring struggle in the city, where its power been has been so long pernicious and so long overwhelming! We rejoice that our opponents have come to the poll and exhausted their utmost effort in behalf of their candidate, because it has revealed to us their strength as well as our own, and has given us the fullest assurance of our entire emancipation.
>
> Twenty thousand independent citizens assembled at the Cross on the day of nomination; they saw their opponents were but a handful; but with the full consciousness of their strength, they did not commit a single outrage upon any individual, or any single act of violence or disorder!

'SO YOU KNOW EDINBURGH?'
A HUNDRED QUESTIONS

1. (a) When was the foundation stone for the Regent Bridge in Waterloo Place laid. (b) who was the Regent? (c) what other name was considered for the structure?

2. (a) Where, in the vicinity of the High Street, can you see former servicemen's married quarters? (b) When were they constructed?

3. Sir Walter Scott was born in College Wynd. The street was demolished, then rebuilt. By what name is it now known?

4. Why do Second World War servicemen have vivid memories of the Music Hall in George Street?

5. What is the proper name for the structure, known as 'Edinburgh's Disgrace', which stands on the Calton Hill?

6. The Krames was a narrow arcade in the High Street, but where precisely was it located?

7. Which building occupies the site of the former New Picture House in Princes Street?

8. What would you buy in a gundy house?

9. By which name was Churchill (the street!) known previously?

10. Who instigated the erection of the Wallace and Bruce memorials at the entrance to Edinburgh Castle?

11. In which year did work start on the Castle Terrace car-park?

12. Where was St Margaret's or, as it was also known, Queen's Station, located?

13. Why is King's Road so named?

14. To whom was George IV speaking when he addressed him as: 'The man in Scotland I most wish to see'?

15. Edinburgh streets have been blessed with curious names, but which one (unofficially) was known as Cut-throat Lane?

16. Can you identify the object shown in the picture above, and describe what practical use it served?

17. There are five streets which meet to form Main Point. What are their names?

18. Can you name the home ports which served the Union Canal?

19. What were the names of the last four ferries which sailed on the Queensferry crossing?

20. Which Leith-born policeman was featured in an edition of the popular television programme *This is Your Life*?

21. Where was Slateford Fever Hospital located?

22. Which specialist city firm supplied clothing for the Scottish Antarctic Expedition of 1902–04?

23. Did the former Edinburgh Corporation tramway system extend outwith the city boundary?

24. Where, not far from Princes Street, will you find the Albert Hall?

25. By what name would older generations of Edinburgh and Leith citizens know the Northern General Hospital?

26. What had Rosehall, Echo Bank, Powburn, Liberton Dams, Nether Liberton, Cameron Toll, Parkneuk and Bridgend in common?

27. Can you describe the contents of the coat-of-arms of the former Burgh of Leith?

28. Which pleasant walk to the south side of the city centre was jocularly referred to as the 'Academic Grove'?

29. Who donated the McEwan Hall in Teviot Place, and in which year did it open?

30. In the late 19th century, when Portobello was a burgh in its own right, it enjoyed two unofficial titles. Can you name them?

31. What was commonly referred to as 'the reaper of the seas'?

32. Why was St Cecilia's Hall in Niddry Street so named?

33. Above the entrance to which busy public building, not far from the High Street, will you see the inscription shown in the picture above?

34. In what special way, in 1967, did the postal service recognise the Edinburgh Festival and the city?

35. Why was the Usher Hall rejected when Admiral Sir David Beatty was granted the freedom of Edinburgh in 1919?

36. What information could be gleaned from Murray's *Edinburgh Diary*?

37 To what use would you put Jacob's Ladder and where is it located?

38. Why is Professor James Gregory so fondly remembered by many of Edinburgh's older citizens?

39. Who described Edinburgh women as 'the best dressed ladies in the Kingdom?

40. The Dean Bridge was erected in 1832, but how long did it take to erect a plaque acknowledging this important fact?

41. Where, on the west side of the town and not far from Haymarket, is there a passageway which bears the bizarre name of 'Coffin Lane'?

42. What common connection have Laurel, Violet, Primrose, Myrtle and Ivy with Edinburgh?

43. Where is the Lockhart Bridge located?

44. A galleon is featured on the roof of George Watson's College, Colinton Road, but where was it displayed previously?

45. Edinburgh had many 'characters' over the centuries, but who, well within living memory, was popularly referred to as Willie Y.?

46. The former Waverley Market in Princes Street had many and varied uses during its long life, but to what use was it put during the First World War?

47. Which famous animal, at one time popular in films, walked on the stairs of the Caledonian Hotel in Princes Street?

48. Where will you find: (a) The Queen's walk? (b) The Queen's Drive? (c) The Duke's Walk?

49. Who was the queen who is remembered by the name 'Queen Street'?

50. Why was the Radical Road constructed?

51. What happened to the criminal prisoners and debtors who were in custody when the old prison in the High Street was demolished in 1817?

52. Prince Alfred, son of Queen Victoria, spent several months in Edinburgh. What was the purpose of this visit?

53. What coincidental connection did Sir Victor Warrender have with the name of a well-known local authority school?

54. Why should Edinburgh residents have a particular interest in the popular TV puffer *Vital Spark*?

55. When was the first breathalyser conviction in Edinburgh?

56. Was it Edinburgh or Leith that won the battle for the first Woolworth shop in the area?

57. Which city clock, in central Edinburgh, originally played music?

58. Did the one o'clock gun and time ball operate during the war years?

59. In which year did Piershill Barracks close?

60. Who (well within living memory) was popularly known as the Lord Provost of Portobello?

61. Where, in a street not far from the West End, was the Poole's Synod Hall located?

62. What location is commonly referred to as 'the windy steps'?

63. There is a round tower at the Lothian Road entrance to St Cuthbert's church. What purpose did it serve originally?

64. What disaster, at the Empire Theatre in 1911, resulted in the cancellation of an historic theatrical occasion?

65. In which busy service concourse, not far from Princes Street, is there a plaque which serves as a reminder of the location of the Physic Garden, a forerunner of the Botanic Garden?

66. Where would you find the 'T' wood?

67. Which cinema was popularly known as 'The Bam' and when did it close?

68. Why, traditionally, is the 'NB' clock kept slightly fast?

69. When did work commence on building Wester Hailes?

70. Where in Peffermill Road, was the 'tin' school located, and why was it so called?

71. Which building was known to Edinburgh housewives as '92'?

72. Can you name three 'Christians' in the vicinity of Portobello?

73. Where was the Gaumont cinema located and what happened to it?

74. What is the Auld Hundred?

75. When were bus lanes introduced?

76. Where was Edinburgh's first Chinese Restaurant located?

77. What was the *Mercurius Politicus*?

78. In which street is the Playhouse Theatre located and what religious building stood on the site previously?

79. Where, within living memory, could be seen the remains of a tree reputedly planted by Mary, Queen of Scots?

80. Which street in Leith, now re-named, was originally called after an Edinburgh Lord Provost?

81. How long did it take to build George IV Bridge?

82. What was popularly known as 'the divi'?

83. Who was known as 'the man in the black coat'?

84. What was 'The Original House of Lords' and why did so many people welcome its existence?

85. Why, in 1945, was the decision taken to display the message 'Our Finest Hour' on the floral clock?

86. Can you describe the Marchmont Circle, and what practical purpose it served?

87. Where and what was Stoneyport?

88. What stands on the site of the John Ker church at Polwarth?

89. Why, in 1645, did the university desert the city and move to Linlithgow for a temporary period?

90. In 1894 a temporary wooden 'hospital' was erected in Holyrood Park. Why?

91. The Waverley Market Carnival was for a very long time a popular attraction during the festive season, but when did this tradition commence?

92. Where and what is Knockillbraehead?

93 Which famous Edinburgh firm was known by the popular name' The Dummie'?

94. What is the interpretation of Edinburgh's motto: NISI DOMINUS FRUSTRA?

95. There was a bandstand in Princes Street Gardens as early as 1877 but what happened to it?

96. What, in local government circles, was known as the 'Greetin' Meetin' '?

97. Where was the author Arthur Conan Doyle born?

98. Can you name the first theatre to be located on the site of the present Festival Theatre in Nicolson Street?

99. When did Holyrood House officially become known as the Palace of Holyroodhouse, and on whose instruction was the change made?

100. Where in London, will you find Edinburgh?

A HUNDRED ANSWERS

1. (a) 1815; (b) The future George IV (then the Prince Regent); (c) Waterloo Bridge (intended as a war memorial).

2. (a) Johnston Terrace (named after Lord Provost William Johnston who was Edinburgh's first citizen 1848–51); (b) 1873.

3. Guthrie Street (in memory of the Revd Thomas Guthrie who died on 24 February 1875).

4. Here, they reported for their 'medical'. Most left the building in the knowledge that they were physically fit — and that their 'calling-up' papers would arrive in due course!

5. The National Monument. The foundation stone was laid on 27 August 1822 during the visit of George IV, although the King was not present at the ceremony. For this duty he appointed the Duke of Atholl, Lords Rosebery, Lyndoch and Elgin. The Duke of Hamilton, as Grand Master Mason, presided over the Masonic ceremonials. It had been hoped to construct an edifice, similar to the Parthenon in Greece at an estimated cost of £60, 000. As contributions amounted to only £15,000 and each column cost an estimated £1,000, the scheme was abandoned.

6. Between the north side of St Giles' Cathedral and the Luckenbooths.

7. The Marks and Spencer store.

8. Sweeties. Gundy was made from treacle and spices.

9. Napier Terrace.

10. Captain Hugh Reid who, in 1854, donated £1,000 for this purpose. The statues were unveiled in 1929 to mark the 600th anniversary of Bruce granting a Charter to the city.

11. 1962 (January). After completion it was available, free of charge, on a first-come basis until 9 September 1964.

12. At Meadowbank, about 100 yards west of where the railway line goes under the road. Possibly it was a convenient stopping point for the Royal Family visiting the palace.

13. It was the route taken by George IV when he reviewed the troops on Portobello sands on 23 August 1822.

14. Sir Walter Scott when they met on the royal yacht on 14 August 1822. Scott had been knighted on 1 April 1820 and was the first baronet created after the King's accession.

15. On the line of what is now Station Road, Gilmerton. This thoroughfare acquired a bad reputation for being the haunt of robbers.

16. It is a link-extinguisher and dates back to the period when street lighting was poor, roads in disrepair and rubbish cluttered the pavements. A wealthy citizen would hire a man to guide him home. He carried a flare to light the way and at the journey's end the 'hire' extinguished his light (to save fuel) in the link-extinguisher outside the house. The ornate one shown in the photograph is located in Melville Street. Other examples can be seen in Charlotte Square and York Place (and no doubt elsewhere).

17. West Port, Lauriston Street, High Riggs, Fountainbridge and Bread Street.

18. Port Hamilton and Port Hopetoun.

19. Queen Margaret, Robert the Bruce, Mary Queen of Scots and Sir William Wallace. The last sailing took place on 4 September 1964, when the road bridge came into use.

20. William Merrilees, who rose to be Chief Constable of Lothians and Peebles Constabulary. He was appointed a constable in Edinburgh City Police on 9 September 1924, and had risen to the rank of Detective Chief Superintendent in 1947. He was appointed Chief Constable of the Lothians and Peebles on 16 May 1950. In 1959 he was awarded the OBE for outstanding voluntary work.

21. Immediately to the south of Slateford railway station.

22. Greensmith Downes who supplied their trademarked 'Australlama' garments for the explorers. The expedition was led by William Spiers Bruce who studied medicine at the University of Edinburgh. The expedition sailed on the *Scotia*. Bruce died in 1921.

23. Yes. For example the Number 21 ran from the Post Office by way of Portobello and Joppa to the terminus at Levenhall.

24. In Shandwick Place. It was built about 1876 as an art gallery. Above the entrance there is the face of Albert in base-relief.

25. Leith Public Health Hospital. It was built just over a century ago.

26. They were hamlets located on the south side of the city.

27. The Virgin and Holy Child seated in the middle of a galley with the motto 'Persevere'. Leith was annexed by Edinburgh more than 70 years ago.

28. The Meadows Walk, because of the number of professional men who lived in the vicinity and consequently walked in the area to places such as the university and the infirmary.

29. William McEwan, MP, at a cost of £110,000, and it opened on 3 December 1897. An honorary degree of LL.D was conferred on him. It is said that he was also acknowledged in an unusual way, his portrait being included in a panel to the right of the platform. On 22 October 1897 McEwan was granted the Freedom of Edinburgh in recognition of his gift.

30. The Scottish Brighton and Edinburgh-on-the-Sea.

31. The Newhaven fishing fleet.

32. After the patron saint of music. The building, located at the foot of Niddry Street, was constructed in 1762.

33. Above the entrance to the public library, George IV Bridge. The quotation is from Genesis, Chapter 1, Verse 3: 'And God said, Let there be light; and there was light'.

    The first attempt to introduce the Public Libraries Act was defeated by 1,106 to 71 votes, the decision being declared on 18 May 1868. On 5 February 1881 it was again rejected — 7,619 voted 'yes' and 15,708 said 'no'. In 1886 Andrew Carnegie offered £25,000 towards the cost of building and equipping a public library. Later that year he sent a cablegram doubling this amount and at a public meeting held in October, 'chaired' by Lord Provost Sir Thomas Clark, the offer was accepted. Carnegie laid the foundation stone on 9 July 1887. Temporary premises were in Hanover Street. Hew Morrison was appointed Principal Librarian in June 1887 and on 9 June

1890 Lord Rosebery formally opened the library. Today we have the Central, 24 community, four mobile, one hospital and one prison library.

34. They issued a special cover to mark the 21st anniversary of the Festival. It also marked the 200th anniversary of the New Town by using the city coat-of-arms for the franking.

35. It was considered to be too small, and the ceremony was held in the Waverley Market. Four thousand guests attended this historic occasion.

36. Mainly train and steamer times. It was first published in 1842 and went out of circulation in 1966. It had a purple cover and was popular because it could slip into a man's waistcoat pocket.

37. The flight of steps which lead from Regent Road (to the east of St Andrew's House) to Calton Road.

38. For his well-known Gregory's Mixture, used for stomach complaints.

39. Charles Jenner, joint-founder of the world-famous Princes Street department store.

40. It took 125 years. It was built by Thomas Telfer at the expense of Lord Provost John Learmonth, who owned the land to the north of the Water of Leith. The plaque was provided by the Institute of Civil Engineers in 1957 to mark the bi-centenery of the designer's birth. Telfer was the Institute's first President.

41. It runs between Dalry Road and Dundee Street to the east of Dalry Cemetery.

42. They are all terraces adjacent to Slateford Road.

43. Spanning the Union Canal at Ashley Terrace. It opened in 1904 and is probably named after the Merchiston councillor, Robert Arthur Lockhart, who died in June 1904.

44. It was taken from the former Watson's College which stood in Archibald Place (off Lauriston Place).

45. Sir William Y. Darling, the well-known Princes Street businessman. He was Lord Provost (1941–44) and later became a Member of Parliament. Sir William is remembered for his flamboyant mode of dress.

46. It was used for the manufacture of tank parts.

47. Trigger, Roy Roger's horse in 1954. The horse was kept at the St Cuthbert's Co-op stables in Grove Street.

48. (a) At the Thistle Foundation complex, Niddrie; (b) Holyrood Park; (c) Also at Holyrood Park. It is a continuation of the Queen's Drive, near St Margaret's Loch, leading to Meadowbank Terrace.

49. Queen Charlotte, wife of George III.

50. Mainly to provide work for unemployed people.

51. The criminal prisoners were transferred to Calton Jail. The twelve debtors were released, their dues having been paid off by way of donations from considerate citizens.

52. He and Prince William of Hesse arrived in the city on 6 October 1863 for the purpose of studying at the university. The Prince spent the winter here and took up residence at Holyrood.

53. When, in 1924, Sir Victor was elevated to the peerage, he adopted the title Lord Bruntsfield of Boroughmuir.

54. A puffer, previously named *Auld Reekie*, was used during filming.

55. On 15 November 1967. There were two cases and fines of £27 and £30 respectively, were imposed. The drivers were also disqualified for twelve months.

56. Leith — by two years, with the store opening in 1924.

57. The one located at the corner of Fraser's store at the West End. The tunes were 'Scotland the Brave' and 'Caller Herrin' '.

58. The use of the gun was suspended for obvious reasons, but 'the ball' provided a time check for those who remembered to look.

59. In 1934; the barracks had been on the site since 1793. The area is now covered by Piershill Square.

60. Councillor Archibald Jameson, who represented the Portobello Ward between 1954–67.

61. Castle Terrace. It was demolished in the mid-to-late 1960s to make way for an opera house. The site is now occupied by Saltire Court, an office block.

62. The steps at the east end of Princes Street which lead to the Waverley Station. This area is notorious for its troublesome wind.

63. It was used as a watch-tower, where men were on duty to protect newly buried corpses from the body-snatchers.

64. A major fire resulted in a Gala Performance, called by George V, being cancelled.

65. The Waverley Station, on the wall facing Platform 11.

66. Near Swanston on the Pentland Hills.

67. The Alhambra, Leith, which closed on 8 March 1958.

68. Allegedly to make passengers hurry along for their trains.

69. January, 1967.

70. It stood approximately opposite Peffermill House and acquired the name because it was constructed from metal.

71. No. 92 Fountainbridge; the main office for the Co-op.

72. Christian Crescent, Christian Grove and Christian Path. They are named after Major Hugh Christian who was Provost of Portobello twice during the 1880s. He was a career soldier who fought in the Indian Mutiny.

73. It was located in Canning Street and destroyed by fire on 30 May 1962. It had been known previously as the Rutland.

74. A Rose Street public-house, appropriately located at No. 100.

75. In 1974. They first appeared in Earl Grey Street.

76. At the George IV Bridge end (south side) of Chambers Street. It was there in the 1930s.

77. A 17th-century newspaper published in London and reprinted in Leith.

78. Greenside Place. The Tabernacle, a Baptist Church with a capacity of 4,000. It was later used as a furniture warehouse.

79. At Little France, not far from Craigmillar Castle.

80. Iona Street. It had been known previously as Falshaw Street, in honour of Sir Thomas Falshaw who was Lord Provost between 1874 and 1877.

81. Nine years; it was completed in 1836. The delay had been caused by the lack of funds!

82. The dividend paid out by the Co-op. It was a blessing for many mothers who relied on this 'wind-fall' to purchase winter clothing for the children.

83. This was a Newhaven expression used to describe a minister of religion.

84. A well known brand of whisky which had Leith connections.

85. To mark the end of the second world war.

86. It was a popular tram route (Number 6) which, as the name suggests, travelled in a circular route. It was very much used by businessmen who lived in the area and also by students.

87. It was a landing stage on the Union Canal and was located at Redhall.

88. Residential flats known as John Ker Court.

89. To avoid the plague which had broken out in the town. One of the most quoted areas affected was Mary King's Close, located beneath the present City Chambers, but at that time it was a narrow, high and congested area.

90. There was a serious out-break of small-pox and the medical facilities were unable to cope with this extra demand. By using the park, it meant that the patients were isolated and therefore reduced the chance of the disease spreading.

91. 23 December 1885.

92. A pedestrian passageway linking Lanark Road (at Kingsknowe) with Colinton.

93. The Edinburgh and Dumfriesshire Dairy Co. Ltd. Their vans and teams of messengers were a familiar sight in the town.

94. It is based on Psalm 127: 'Except the Lord build the house, they labour in vain that build it: except the Lord keep the city, the watchman waketh but in vain'.

95. It was removed to the Meadows and eventually demolished in 1953.

96. The last meeting before the elections!

97. At No. 11 Picardy Place.

98. The Edinburgh Empire Palace Theatre of Varieties which opened on 7 November 1892.

99. In March 1929 on an opinion expressed by King George V.

100. At Tottenham Hotspur FC. They have a player on their books called Justin Edinburgh!